# CATFIGHT IN THE KITCHEN

and other ruminations on animals, pets, and spirituality

Note for Librarians: A cataloguing record for this book is available from Library
and Archives Canada at www.collectionscanada.ca/amicus/index-e.html

Printed in Victoria, BC, Canada.

ISBN: 978-1-4251-5997-9

*We at Trafford believe that it is the responsibility of us all, as both individuals
and corporations, to make choices that are environmentally and socially sound.
You, in turn, are supporting this responsible conduct each time you purchase a
Trafford book, or make use of our publishing services. To find out how you are
helping, please visit www.trafford.com/responsiblepublishing.html*

*Our mission is to efficiently provide the world's finest, most comprehensive
book publishing service, enabling every author to experience success.
To find out how to publish your book, your way, and have it available
worldwide, visit us online at www.trafford.com/10510*

www.trafford.com

**North America & international**
toll-free: 1 888 232 4444 (USA & Canada)
phone: 250 383 6864 ♦ fax: 250 383 6804
email: info@trafford.com

**The United Kingdom & Europe**
phone: +44 (0)1865 722 113 ♦ local rate: 0845 230 9601
facsimile: +44 (0)1865 722 868 ♦ email: info.uk@trafford.com

10 9 8 7 6 5 4 3

*Dedicated* to my dear wife and children, each of whom are inspirations to me.

# TABLE OF CONTENTS

# PREFACE

*S*ix things I have seen in twenty-first century North America, seven that boggle the mind. An openness to spirituality, a distrust of organized religion, unprecedented materialism, an interest in animals and pets, a search for truth, eagerness to explore alternative ways of thinking, and yet staunch resistance to change.

I find myself in that strange land of contradictions, searching for truth yet hesitant lest I find it and the consequences are too much to bear. Still, something greater draws me onward and my amazement of the created order turns me to the miracle of life itself. Life—of which I am a part but next to which I find myself so small. Humbled, I am able to look to lesser life for greater truth. Able to exult in the variety of created living beings, interacting with me.

As a veterinarian I have had the privilege of experiencing a variety of intersection of human and animal life in a more intimate way than many, and in so doing, have seen much. I am repeatedly astonished at the significant contribution that "dumb" animals make to the quality of life of their caretakers. It has been humbling to see over and over again how much there is to learn from creatures we think of as belonging to us.

The tales in this little book all come from my personal experiences. I am not pretending to be an expert and I know that I have a lot more to learn than many. I do, however, wish to share with you some tales of companion animals and their caretakers whom I have met over the years. The first group of chapters contain stories from my veterinary work, starting from early in my North American career and followed by several that arose from experiences overseas. Secondly there are some narratives dealing with "the mundane and the miraculous," starting off with a few tales told from the perspective of the animals involved. Finally, the last set of chapters (part three) offers information and suggestions for present and prospective pet owners. In all cases, names of pets and their owners have been changed to conceal their identities.

My hope first of all is that you will enjoy the stories themselves. If there is any insight gained from them, so much the better. If you find this book an aid in your spiritual journey, thank not the writer but the Giver of life.

Spirituality. Animals. What do these topics have in common? Read on.

# INTRODUCTION

*C*onsider the flowers...consider the birds...consider our pets.

Many people think spirituality is a topic not related to animals. Those who feel that way however, are usually not pet owners! There certainly is a lot more to our pets than meets the eye.

Most of us have noticed that pets can make wonderful companions and friends. They can be great teachers as well. But have you ever wondered why? What is it about our special friends that we find so attractive and comforting? Why is it that we often feel more free to share our thoughts with a pet than with friends, family and sometimes even a spouse? I have heard people say they feel more comfortable telling the dog their problems than praying to God about them! Why is that? If we can find out why, could we perhaps emulate our pets in some positive way?

Please do not think I am suggesting that animals are better than people, nor that they are inherently superior. Certainly a few of my clients think so, and I must admit that if pressed I would have to say that some animals act in a more "humane" way than some people. Sometimes!

A number of people have given me feedback on the question of why they find it easier to talk to pets than with people. Many say it is because animals do not talk back, and never disagree with you. Others say it is because their pets make no unreasonable demands on them, or that they feel loved by their pets. Well, "love" is a big word, one that needs a clear definition before we can use it in truth and with meaning. That sort of definition is beyond the scope of this book, but well worth considering. I'm sure that we all can agree on this though—there is less negative reaction from animals than from a perhaps more discriminating human audience when we air our views and opinions. No doubt it is safer to express socially unacceptable or inflammatory comments to our pets than to friends and family. However, I think there are a few other reasons why we may be more likely to confide in a pet than in a person.

The first of these reasons is that our pets are on the whole very accepting. No matter what you say you can be sure that in their opinion you are still the next best thing to canned food. Whatever you give they will accept (even if they ignore it), and they do not try to prove themselves superior to you (with cats, that is because their superiority is a known and non-negotiable fact).

The second reason is that our pets always live in the NOW. To the best of their ability, and almost without exception, they seem to forget the past and not worry about tomorrow. They always expect that tomorrow will be at least as good as today and do not see any reason to expect things will deteriorate from where they are right now (which is at worst bearable and at best delightful).

A third reason is obvious—although we do not all agree on just how much our pets can understand we know they are always happy to listen to us! In addition, all of our spilled secrets are safe and will certainly not be re-told. No wonder many consider our animals trusted confidantes—good listeners, reliable secret keepers, non-judgmental, and contented.

Still… maybe the things we tell only our pets say more about ourselves than anybody else.

Regardless, I think there is a lot to say for living in the eternal now, accepting things for how they are, and looking to the future with hope. Without doubt we could do well to emulate our pets. Sometimes!

Most people believe that we humans live in a reality much more full than what we experience only through our five senses. There certainly are dimensions to our pets' existence that science alone cannot explain. It appears to me that animals perceive such reality even more acutely and with less surprise than humans do. Many of us have experienced the sensitivity of animals around autistic and mentally challenged individuals, and the special bonds animals make with some people and other animals are amazing. Animals have traveled through unknown territory over long distances (without a map!) to be re-united with owners who have moved far away. Examples like these abound, and have been documented. Let me give you a few more.

An elderly gentleman had a dog, which he asked a nephew to take care of while he was in the hospital for a while. Unfortunately, the old man died there and so never did come home. The same day his master died, the dog ran away from the nephew's house. Relatives went looking for the dog and several days later found him lying on the elderly gentleman's recently dug grave, in a town many miles away where the dog had never been before.

A woman who lived alone had a cat. The two of them had well-defined routines including cleaning and feeding, but the cat never seemed much for affection or sitting on her lap. Once, when the woman came home after an emotionally trying day, she dissolved into tears, sobbing on the floor. Just then, when she was feeling very alone and vulnerable, her cat came over, lay down beside her, and gently caressed her cheek with his paw.

A young boy began to have seizures when he was seven years old. After thorough testing, the diagnosis was epilepsy. The seizures themselves were not harmful to him, but secondary injuries resulting from seizures were a very real danger. Unfortunately, no one including the boy himself could tell when such an attack was to occur. So he had to always wear protective gear, and greatly limit his activities. It soon became clear, however, that the family dog could sense when a seizure was about to happen. She would run up to the boy, bark, and gently pull on his arm about five minutes before a seizure would start. The boy learned to respond to the dog's warnings by lying down in a safe place whenever she alerted him to an impending seizure. The dog was so reliable and accurate with her warnings that the boy was able to resume a generally normal life style whenever she was with him.

Animals seem to have the remarkable ability to sense natural disasters or severe weather changes more accurately than we, even with all our technological advances. Sometimes we ascribe that to chance, sometimes to luck. But could it be that our pets might show sensitivities to spiritual realities that we are often too dull to notice? Are they participating in a very real world that we somehow tend to ignore?

This type of thinking brings to mind a story of a lamb lost in a big city. No one knew where it came from or what to do about it. It surprised everyone so much to see a lamb in the concrete jungle that no one did anything to help. The lamb wandered around the streets, finally ending up in a central square area where there was a statue. A leaky drinking fountain was there as well, with water trickling down to form a small pool at its base. Around the bottom, through cracks in the concrete, grew tufts of green. The tired, hungry lamb drank greedily, and eagerly munched the grass. It wandered over to the statue and lay down to rest. To the passerby it was a lonely, lost and pathetic animal. The lamb, however, was lying in green pastures beside still waters.

Truth can indeed be stranger than fiction.

# PART 1
# VETERINARY VIGNETTES

# 1 STRANGE REASONING

*Some* lessons just have to be learned the hard way— things are not always as they seem.

One of my professors in Veterinary College was fond of telling his classes, "More things are missed because of not looking than because of not knowing." In other words, we were to always remember to be thorough in our physical examinations. Our schooling trained us to rely heavily on our physical senses when performing a physical exam. The only sense on which we do not rely of course, is taste; sight, sound, touch and smell however are all important in coming to an appreciation of any abnormalities in a patient. Another factor in reaching a diagnosis that can be just as important as the physical exam in many cases, is the history of health problems as relayed by a pet owner. By "history" I mean information such as how long the ailment has been going on, what the first abnormality noted was, what other changes there have been, and so forth.

That is why, when performing a health evaluation in our patients, we ask for historical and background information in addition to carefully examining a pet and using whatever other diagnostic tools we need. The desire to help sick animals get better is one of the main reasons people bring their pets to a veterinarian; this is the primary reason people like me even want to become veterinarians. So it was with some consternation that I could not find out what was wrong with Mr. Dumfries' dog. I had just graduated with my Doctor of Veterinary Medicine degree and was eager to put into practice all the things I had learned in my classes and residency. Yet no matter what I did we could not find out what Jupiter's illness was, much less find an appropriate therapy to control the scratching that she was doing at home.

It started out innocently enough—Mr. Dumfries had phoned the clinic where I was a newly hired associate vet and booked an appointment to get his dog Jupiter checked for a "skin ailment". She had been scratching ever since she was a young pup he said, and it was getting worse. Several months earlier she had been spayed. According to the medical records, there was no history of any scratching or skin problem at that time. My physical examination of Jupiter revealed no abnormalities either. There was no indication of redness, no sign of swelling, no hint of hair loss, and no suggestion of scratch marks. When I told Mr. Dumfries that there were no symptoms associated with skin problems at all, he retorted, "Are you going to believe me or not, son? She needs help and if you can't give it to her here I will just have to take her elsewhere." I hurriedly assured him that if Jupiter was scratching she was scratching, and I would try to help. In most cases, I told him, an underlying dermatologic problem usually shows up as skin lesions. In cases where there are no lesions but scratching is intense, we usually at least see evidence of scratching. Scratching certainly could result from hormonal or behavioral problems that would not result in a sickly looking skin, but this demanded additional testing. We would start with screening blood work and likely progress to skin biopsies and possibly to allergy testing. Mr. Dumfries readily agreed to this. Although he knew the cost of getting a definitive diagnosis might be high, he seemed very committed to doing the best he could for his pet.

The blood analysis results were normal in all respects. The next step, biopsy of the skin, proved to be a bit of a challenge, because the most useful biopsies are those harvested from skin lesions, and Jupiter didn't have any. So we took seven little biopsies from various areas of the body, to be thorough. Despite meticulous microscopic study of each biopsy and additional special histologic staining to detect more unusual problems, the pathologists could find no trace of any abnormalities in the skin tissue.

At this stage I was becoming more than a little frustrated. How was it that despite employing all our knowledge and diagnostic tools we were unable to help poor Jupiter? At the same time I was beginning to doubt the severity of scratching Mr. Dumfries reported, as I had never actually seen it nor any sign of its cause nor its effects! Mr. Dumfries was adamant, however, that the problem was not only present, but worsening over time. We placed Jupiter on a hypoallergenic diet to see if that would help, and tested her for inhaled allergies as well. The results came back—negative. There was no evidence of abnormal reactions to any common allergen. Nor was there any response to the special diet.

My veterinary college professor had often said, "More things are missed because of not looking than because of not knowing." With Jupiter, however, we had looked for every possible cause of scratching, and come up with no diagnosis.

Mr. Dumfries was unwilling to accept that there was nothing wrong with his dog and wanted me to give her some medication. I dispensed anti-inflammatory tablets thinking that even though the skin biopsy was normal, there must be <u>something</u> bothering her. The medication did her no good. "Give me anything to stop this terrible scratching," demanded Mr. Dumfries. He seemed to be losing his patience with the situation. In desperation I prescribed sedatives for Jupiter. Finally we had found something that helped. Mr. Dumfries said she responded well to those medications and was hardly scratching at all. Ahhh, I thought—success at last.

For quite a while I saw nothing else of Mr. Dumfries other than him picking up refills of the sedative. Several times I advised him to reduce the dosage to see if we could get Jupiter off medication and each time he reported trying but having to increase the dose again because of recurrent scratching. Then a few weeks later I got a phone call from an exasperated Mrs. Dumfries. "Are you Dr. Kwantes?" she asked. When I said yes she immediately replied, "I am sure you are a nice young man but will you please stop messing with our dog?"

I was shocked. "What do you mean?" I asked. And so the story came out that poor Mr. Dumfries himself had the problem—a psychological one. Apparently he had a severe mite infestation when he was a boy, so that his skin had secondarily become infected from all his scratching and he had almost died. Ever since then he was extremely sensitive to any itch and positively paranoid when he noticed other people scratching.

"I've had to learn to resist the urge to scratch whenever he is with me," Mrs. Dumfries explained, "or he will insist I go to the doctor for a check-up. I discovered this over time, and so now avoid the urge to scratch whenever he is around. But Jupiter does not know this. She is not at all scratching more than any other dog I know, but now that she is on these drugs of yours she is sleeping most of the time and not enjoying life as before. Please don't give my husband any more medications for the poor dog. Let me assure you there is no reason for the medication you are giving Jupiter."

Suddenly everything fit. No wonder I could never find Jupiter's skin problem—I had been treating a phantom illness, one that existed only in the mind of her owner!

Jupiter and her skin "problem" forced me to do some serious self-reflection on some things I took for granted and how I related to people and their pets. Today, based on that episode and others like it I believe my professors sage advice needs to be amended to, "more things are missed for not looking than for not knowing; be as thorough as you can, but remember that things are not always as they seem."

Or are they?

# STANLEY CUP VET

*I* remember it well—my first large animal surgery. Well, not really the very first but it was the first one I performed by myself. Despite all the surgery theory and practice I had at Veterinary College, and no matter how many times I had assisted my veterinary employer in the field, being responsible for recommending and performing my first major solo surgery was a big deal to me. That is one of the reasons I remember it so well. Another reason is that it happened on a very cold spring night, a Stanley Cup night at that. I do not remember who was playing, but I certainly remember thinking the farmyard looked deserted when I came calling.

Earlier that day dairyman Kooiker had phoned about one of his cows who was doing poorly and he wanted it seen right away. The day had been busy for me, with a long list of calls, so by the time I arrived at his empty farmyard it was past 7:00 p.m. Going to the farmhouse door, and hoping I looked so gaunt that Mrs. Kooiker might take pity on me and offer a taste of whatever it was that smelled so good, I knocked, then waited. After a couple of minutes I knocked again, harder. After yet another few minutes of waiting, Mr. Kooiker came out and asked, "What do you want?" I said I had come to check his cow and he said, "You're the vet?" "Yes," I replied. "Well let's get out and have a look at her," he said. "Hurry—the hockey game is on!"

He quickly led me through his barn and pointed out the affected cow. Apparently my physical exam took longer than he wanted it to, because he had disappeared by the time I finished.

Going back to the house, after another few knocks, I explained that his cow had a right-sided displacement of her abomasum (stomach) which required surgical correction to reposition it. "Well, go ahead," he said.

With some fear and trepidation I shaved and prepared the cow for surgery, and infiltrated her skin with a local anesthetic. Cutting into her side and reaching deep within I was able to deflate the bloated stomach, hold it in position, and suture it in place. Later, after suturing the final layer of skin, and feeling elated that all had gone so well, I triumphantly walked back through the now blackened yard and knocked on the farmhouse door again. Three times. Mr. Kooiker finally came to the door and said, "Are you still here?"

"Yes," I replied, "and the surgery is done and all went well!" I then gave him post-surgical instructions, spoken to the back of his head as he craned his neck around the corner trying to watch the game.

A follow-up phone call several days later revealed that the cow was doing well. As Mr. Kooiker was not my regular client it was several months until I saw him again. Walking through his barn that day I asked him how the cow I had done surgery on several months earlier was doing. Stopping and turning to me, he said, "You never did that surgery!" "Sure did!" I countered. "Don't you remember it was a Stanley Cup hockey night?" "Of course I do," he retorted, "but that was not you— don't you know that cow is worth $45,000?! I wouldn't let just anyone touch her!"

So my private triumph needed to remain just that—a personal one, for Mr. Kooiker would not believe it was I who had helped him that night. I learned that no matter how important veterinary work might seem to me, some things just cannot compete with Stanley Cup Fever!

# 3 | MISCONCEPTION

$\mathcal{T}$he two old brothers were a sight to behold, reminiscent of the Beverly Hillbillies. They were some of the last of a dying breed of subsistence dairy farmers who were being driven out of the market by mega-dairies. Bob, 82 years old, and Willie, his younger brother of 78, had owned their small farm for almost thirty years after they purchased it from their Dad just before he passed away.

As the two of them ambled out of the house, Bob with his ever-present cigar stub jammed between his gums and Willie with his limp from a sore hip, I couldn't help thinking that not much had changed on the homestead since the day they started farming. And probably never would, I thought. I had driven out to have a look at some calves with diarrhea. The vet I was working for had diagnosed a Salmonella outbreak several weeks earlier and I was doing the follow-up call. As Willie limped up to my van I could see he was not impressed that a young whippersnapper had come to the farm instead of the older more experienced vet.

"You know about our dog Rex, eh?" he asked. Bob had gone around to chain up Rex, who had a reputation for hiding behind the silo and attacking visitors with gusto. Although Rex now had only as few teeth as Bob, stories had it that in his younger days he had put an unlucky visitor in the hospital for a month. "You bet," I said. My boss, whose leg scars proved that Rex was a serious threat, did warn me ahead of time.

We slowly made our way over frozen ruts and around rusty discarded implements into the dilapidated barn. Stooping into the dimness we carefully avoided the drooping wooden door frame that sunk toward the cracked cement threshold.

In the barn, father and sons walked the same steps for decades. The path, clearly outlined in heaving cement, looked much like one of the cow paths in the field outside.

After looking over the calves I watched the brothers saunter over to the main barn door and call the cows in by name for milking. As each cow ran into her own stall to eat grain, Bob and Willie carried over the milking machines and hooked them up. Once milking was over, they broke out the hay bales and then it was time for morning chores. The two were bemoaning the fact that the milk butterfat percentages were never quite as high as they wanted. Increased milk yields would be nice too but they didn't really want to push the cows too hard. If they could just increase the butterfat percentage though, they would receive a premium price for the milk.

"If you like, I can give you a suggestion," I said. They looked at me as though they had both just become aware of my presence, with quizzical expressions on their stubbled faces. "And what would that be?" Bob asked.

I explained that because they were first feeding a grain supplement at milking time and then later giving the hay, they were actually disrupting normal digestion in the rumen (stomach). Large amounts of grain would make the juices in the rumen quite acidic and that would have a negative effect on the microorganisms that break down the hay. It would be better, I suggested, to feed hay first and grain later. The grain would still provide the same nutrition but have less of an acidifying effect, because the hay in the rumen would have a buffering effect and provide for a better digestion environment.

"We've done it like this for forty years, and we need the grain to entice the cows into the barn," Willy stated, stealing a glance at his big brother. "You sure about that Willy?" replied Bob. "We could give it a try." And they both went back to work.

Months later I had another call to their farm. What an eerie feeling I had, driving into the static farmyard. Not a piece of machinery was out of place, not a thing had moved. Except Rex, chained up and barking like a dog possessed, doing his best to drag the silo over to my van.

The brothers had a cat that needed tending, and I didn't get to see the cows at all that day. My curiosity finally got the better of me. As I was climbing back into the van, I yelled over Rex's commotion to ask Bob, "Tell me, did you ever try feeding hay first instead of grain?"

"Young fella, the cows changed over with a lot less fuss than Willy did. And I'll be darned if our fat level didn't climb up by almost half a percent. Just goes to show that little things do mean a lot. You don't think Willy would have you out to look at his precious cat if you hadn't proved yourself with the cows, do you?"

I had to admit that I had misjudged someone's character yet again. Not only had Bob and Willie proven to have soft hearts under their gruff exteriors, they were probably more willing than myself to take advice from someone who had a whole lot less life experience.

# 4 | LUCKY

There was a real sense of déjà vu, with a twist. Here I was with the Johnsons, putting their cat (aptly named Lucky) to sleep after a short but dramatic illness. Lucky had indeed been fortunate. Four years earlier (named Rocky at the time), his original owners brought him to the veterinary clinic for emergency care. Rocky had been shot through the side of his head. The bullet had gone through his skull and out the eye socket, destroying his left eye. Poor Rocky looked gruesome, but despite his pain he was actually purring while I examined him. Rocky's story was sad and all too common, but the woman who brought Rocky was straightforward and honest.

It all started out with a movie that starred a cat with which the woman's daughter Alana fell in love. Despite repeated attempts by her parents to talk her out of getting a kitten, nothing would appease her. After seeing Alana's efforts to gain information on cats and cat care through literature reviews in the library, her parents finally did get her a kitten. So began a delightful period of infatuation, where Alana doted on the kitten she named Rocky—all was well. As Rocky grew however, some of his dominance tendencies started showing. It rapidly became Rocky rather than Alana who decided when it was time for snuggling, and Rocky rather than Alana who decided when it was playtime. After a few incidents in which Rocky made his will known in no uncertain terms, Alana's interest in Rocky waned rapidly and she turned to other pursuits.

As Alana lost interest in Rocky, so did her commitment to feed and water and play with him. Soon it was her mom and dad who ended up cleaning the kitty litter (it was usually her mother who ended up doing so because whenever the litter was dirty, Rocky would inevitably start urinating in the house, and you know who would always end up cleaning that). Mom became irritated with the cat, Dad did not want anything to do with him, and Alana frankly, didn't care any more.

So it was that Alana and her family had a discussion to determine what to do. Accusations flew, feelings were hurt, and everyone felt badly. Overall, the family thought that Rocky's quality of life was not good, and they decided to find a new home for him. Though that initially seemed like a good idea, it proved very difficult to do. One day, after several weeks of frustration in trying to locate a new home, Alana's father stepped in a wet spot left by Rocky on the carpet. This was the last straw for Dad, so that very day while Mom and Alana were out shopping, he took Rocky and his .22 rifle out for a ride. He let Rocky go in the back of a grain field and shot him. When Mom and Alana came home, Dad at first pretended that Rocky had gone missing. That caused a surprising amount of angst and determination to find him—a lot more than Dad had expected, so he admitted to what he had done. As you can imagine, that landed him in much deeper hot water yet. But the worst of all came four days later, when Rocky showed up at the house again! He was severely injured, hungry and thin, matted and bloody. Despite all his pain, however, he was still looking for care and attention from his adopted family. Aghast, Mom picked him up and brought him to the vet clinic, intending to have him put to sleep.

Surprised that Rocky could overall look so well after sustaining such terrible wounds, I gave him a thorough exam, took radiographs and blood samples. When the results were available, I explained to Alana's mom that a surgery to remove the damaged eye was all that Rocky needed. However, she advised me that no matter what, she wanted me to put Rocky to sleep and that she could and would not be taking him home. I explained to her that another option was available; if she would relinquish all rights to Rocky I would take him and see if I could find another home for him. Alana's mom was unconvinced—how did she know I would be successful? I explained to her that when we viewed the situation from Rocky's perspective, any option other than leaving him as is would be better being put to sleep. She finally agreed and signed the papers, crying as she kissed Rocky good-bye. She paid for the examination and left.

Rocky had narrowly escaped death at the hands of his caretakers. Not having anywhere else to go, he had found his way back home after being abandoned. Now in the clinic, he had a chance to start over again. The eye removal surgery went well, with no complications, and he found a new home at the Johnson house. They re-named him Lucky and doted over him for the next two years.

Other than becoming fatter than he should, things went well for Lucky at the Johnson's. So when he started to refuse food and water, his owners became very concerned. By the second day of not eating he was vomiting too, and very weak. The Johnsons brought Lucky into the clinic for evaluation, where examination revealed he was dehydrated and very pale. Blood work showed that he had marked anemia as well as severe leukemia. Unfortunately, he also tested positive for exposure to Feline Leukemia Virus. This meant that. other than supportive care, there was very little we could do for him. We gave him fluids and anti-inflammatory medication because the Johnsons wanted him to come home for the night, in the hopes he would get better. He did not improve, and the next day the cat and his loving caretakers were back; they spared Lucky the inevitable distress of advancing illness and he passed away gently in the arms of those he trusted.

Within each living being is a desire for life. Yet it is the lot of all living creatures to die eventually. Lucky almost experienced a violent death at the hands of those who ostensibly had his best interest in mind. Indirectly, the previous owners were likely also responsible for his "second" death, as

Lucky probably contracted Feline Leukemia Virus from exposure during his trip back home after being shot. Despite his terrible experience, Lucky (for whatever reason) retained his trust in people and contributed immensely to the Johnson family before finally succumbing to illness. Would that we could all follow the example of Lucky and regardless of hardship, choose life.

# 5 | SURPRISE!

"*P*lease come quickly," Keith said, and even over the phone I could tell by the tone of his voice how very worried he was.

You wouldn't think it of the tall, handsome, well-known socialite, but there he was on his knees in the corner of the garage. He was crawling on the dirty cement floor, offering a milk-soaked piece of bread to a frightened half-wild kitten. "Look at him! He can hardly walk," Keith cried, tears forming in his eyes. I could see right away that the kitten was in agony. When I tried to get a closer look, fear overrode pain and the terrified creature took off like a shot. It had an irregular gait that looked more like a bear walking on loose rocks than an agile member of the cat family.

"What can we do?" Keith asked. He then proceeded to tell me that for the last few weeks he had been trying to tame the wild kitten that showed up on his doorstep one day. "I think it was dropped off in the neighborhood by someone—it certainly doesn't trust humans." Keith had hoped to take the kitten in as a house cat but found that to be a big challenge. He was making some headway and was able to stay with the kitten while it ate the food he gave, but so far he had not been able to touch it.

This morning he noticed the kitten just sitting on its haunches looking depressed. On closer inspection he noticed that there was swelling and a whitish discoloration of the footpads. Sure enough, when I observed the location where the kitten had been sitting there were small wet spots on the cement where its feet had been. That concerned me. Most likely the poor thing was suffering from severe pad irritation due to chemical or thermal burns. It was also possible the kitten had an autoimmune disease that was causing blister development on its feet. But how in the world could we catch the poor creature, much less treat it? Keith had tried luring it into a cat carrier but there was no way it would even come near anything remotely strange.

We devised a plan to trick the cat into being caught. Keith started leaving its food in the neck of a large pottery jar. A few days later, while it was eating, the kitten received the second biggest surprise of its life (the first being whatever caused its feet injuries). Keith and I sprung an ambush. While the kitten was eating, it suddenly found himself trapped in the pot, then surrounded by a towel, and tightly wrapped. His surprise was so great that I doubt he felt the prick from the tranquilizing needle with which I injected him. A few minutes later he was blissfully unaware while I examined him. I treated his damaged feet by applying burn cream on the blisters and bandaging them. I also administered an injection of long-acting antibiotics. We needed to keep him under sedation for several days to change bandages and give further treatment; after that he was free to go. It was a real treat to see Agnes (Keith gave him a girl's name—don't ask me why) slowly get better, and his steady growth was the best reward for helping him.

Over time Agnes learned to trust Keith to a large degree, and even felt comfortable enough to move into the house. Although Agnes never lost his careful nature and distrust of new people, he shared a new found companionship with Keith, who also had the pleasure of knowing he had helped change Agnes' life forever.

The lessons that this story illustrates are many, but the most obvious is that patience and love is enough to win the heart of most creatures. As caretakers of animals, let us always aim to treat them as the gifts they are.

Abandoned animals have it rough so please never abandon a pet! If you are unable for any reason to give your pet the care it deserves please take it somewhere where it will at least have its basic needs met. Remember that even in difficult situations your veterinarian may be able to help alleviate suffering in animals. Ask for help.

# 6 SKUNKED!

*A* strange position to be in, to say the least—nose to nose with a frightened skunk. A client had called early that morning to say he had a big challenge for me. During the night a skunk had tried to crawl through a hole in the wall of his garage, but had become stuck part way. Its head was on the inside, its body on the outside, and its back end was pointing at the house. It looked completely stressed out, to put it mildly.

Which is exactly how I would describe the man and his wife (the wife left for a friend's house shortly after I arrived). The level of stress and fear of both skunk and man was directly related to the angle the skunk held its tail above the ground.

"I found him that way this morning when I got up," he told me, "and couldn't decide if it was better to approach this problem head on or sneak up from behind. In the end I thought better of either approach and decided to phone you."

Not having training or experience in skunk management, I decided to have a closer look at the head of the skunk, since the back end seemed fine. While I slowly approached the head on the inside, the unhappy garage owner stood outside and kept me updated as to how high the tail was. Presumably, the higher the tail the more likely the skunk would be to spray—we were fortunate it had not done so already! Without making the skunk or the man too nervous, I was able to ascertain that the skunk was uninjured except for skin irritation on its neck. This must have been from pulling against the wall while trying to back up and squeeze out the hole. There was little blood loss and the damage was only skin deep, so we decided to extract the skunk. A quick phone call to Department of Fish and Wildlife gave us permission to do so. They did not regard rabies as a concern in this case, since there were no signs of abnormal behavior, and no reports of a skunk bite.

I brought out some liquid anesthetic, normally used in gas anesthetic machines. There was no way I could put equipment such as a gas mask close to the skunk's face while it was wide awake. Using a syringe, I carefully squirted some anesthetic liquid in front of its head, always mindful of the tail position update being shouted from the other side of the wall. The lower the tail, the closer I could approach and the more anesthetic the skunk would breathe. Slowly but surely the skunk became more and more relaxed, until it was not aware of anything that was happening. We carefully placed the skunk's back end in a plastic bag (just in case), and ever so gently I twisted its head to the point where it could be pushed back through the hole. A quick application of ointment on the affected skin, and we carried him out to a nearby field and let him go (downwind).

We had hoped that the stress of waking up from anesthetic in a different place than where he went to sleep would not frighten the skunk too much. There were a few tense moments for us as he woke up and staggered a little before heading off into the bush. Once he was out of our sight and we started breathing again we realized that there was not even a whiff of skunk smell in the air or in the garage. Amazing! Patience and a gentle touch had won the day again.

And I had forgotten my camera!!

# 7 | TOUGH GUY

*He* swaggered into the clinic, his python draped around his neck. The two-meter long snake rode into the exam room, flicking its tongue rapidly. "Can you help my snake, Doc? His name is Bruno and I think he has some sort of skin problem."

I took the snake from him, firmly grasping it at the base of its head. Its color was not right, and the general attitude was one of depression. Bruno's body condition was poor, and he had a mild but distinctly offensive odor about him. As I was examining the snake and came to the middle of his body, I could tell that my touch was causing pain. On his underside his abdomen was swollen and reddened, the scales were separating and there was a discharge oozing between them. The poor animal was suffering from a severe skin infection that was draining the body of fluid and protein and also causing pain and suffering.

The owner, who really did want the best for his snake, was shocked to learn of the severity of Bruno's condition. "How long has he been like this?" I asked. "Well, he hasn't been eating for about six months, and he was a bit off a few months ago. He never did seem to get completely better but I thought he was mostly OK until a few days ago when I saw the scales looking funny. Can you do anything?"

We talked about possible causes of Bruno's infection, took samples to get laboratory confirmation of the type of infection and the best antibiotic to use, and discussed environmental changes and management improvements the owner would have to make. "I didn't think it would be this complicated," he said. "And I don't have the money to do the recommended testing, either."

In veterinary practice we often need to deal with the frustration of basing treatment on a tentative diagnosis only, as the cost of doing a proper medical work-up is more than some clients are willing to pay. In this case, although the prognosis for Bruno was poor, we initiated therapy and the owner said he would change the lighting, housing, and feeding of his python.

"A couple other thoughts," I said. "First of all, I know a few people who would get quite a scare if you walked past them with a big snake hanging over your shoulders and it got close to them. Also, people can get infections from reptiles, and in fact the discharge from your snake could be loaded with Salmonella, a bacteria that can cause serious intestinal disease and even death in people. Please wash your hands very carefully between touching your snake and anything else. And it would be wise not to let anyone else handle him until he is better."

He got the message—as I walked into the next exam room I could see him bent over a back sink, scrubbing his own neck with antibiotic soap! He followed up by doing a lot of reading about requirements of taking proper care of exotic pets, and ended up with a scarred but healthy Bruno, plus several other thriving reptile friends!

In my experience with reptiles and other exotic pets (and dogs and cats), one of the most sensitive indicators I know to suggest illness in a pet is the impression of a perceptive owner that something is wrong. When owners have a good appreciation of what to expect with pets and an appreciation for what is normal for an individual animal, they often can tell very quickly that something is wrong. That is when we say that an animal has a condition called ADR—"ain't doin' right!" Often a physical exam and some simple lab testing can diagnose the problem. The earlier we reach a diagnosis, the earlier we can start appropriate therapy and the more likely we are to achieve a good result. So whether you are looking for some disease prevention advice or whether you have a pet that has ADR, a phone call or visit to your local veterinary clinic can help both you and your pet.

# 8 | REASON TO HOPE

$\mathscr{P}$ets are great for kids! For adults, too. However, some of life's hard learning experiences for both children and adults come as a result of having pets. Pets sometimes start out as dearly loved companions but later prove to be a frustration.

A young couple was looking for a good pet for their four-year old son. They knew that rabbits do not make the best pets for young children, yet when they saw some lovely gentle rabbits at a friend's house they decided to get one for the boy. They found a rabbit breeder (funny how we call people breeders when it is the animals that are doing the breeding) who had a lot of rabbits which all ran around in an enclosed area on his farm. Although the bunnies seemed scared, the man assured the parents that no one ever complained about temperament problems with his rabbits. They bought a cute little brown bunny and named him Brownie. At first things went well, but of course responsibility of caring for Brownie fell onto the shoulders of the boy's parents. Soon, although he professed to love him, the boy became disinterested in spending time with Brownie. Things became worse when the rabbit started showing signs of aggression and soon nobody could even take him out of the cage without risk of injury. The boy's parents had made a commitment to their pet how-ever, so they brought the rabbit into the veterinary clinic to check for health problems. They also had him neutered, because neutering will sometimes help control aggression in male rabbits.

Even after being neutered, there was not much change in Brownie's attitude. Because the family figured fresh air would be good for him, they often brought Brownie outside to spend time in an enclosure in the yard. Another well-loved family pet, a small dog, at first showed some interest in Brownie but over time paid no attention to him either. The parents felt sorry that neither man nor beast was interested in Brownie, and they insisted the boy spend more time with his rabbit. When Brownie scratched the boy twice, however, he became afraid of the rabbit. One day and for no apparent reason, the rabbit bit the boy on his ear as he carried him outside. The injury was serious enough to warrant a trip to the doctor. The wound was not serious enough to need sutures, but the doctor did prescribe antibiotic therapy.

This incident led to a serious family discussion. It was bad enough that Brownie stomped his feet and resisted being picked up, but the parents were not about to allow him to be a health hazard for their son. They decided they would have to get rid of the rabbit and learn from the experience. No one, however, expressed interested in adopting a rabbit with a history of aggression. A phone call to the SPCA confirmed that the chance of someone taking a vicious rabbit was about zero, and most likely it would end up being put to sleep. A phone call to their veterinarian revealed there was no one they knew of looking for a rabbit either. Again, the fact that he was not tame meant that chances of someone taking him were very slim.

Fortunately, the family lived in a relatively secluded acreage, and there were other rabbits that lived in the woods. The neighbors all thought they were wild rabbits even though they did not look like hares. Everyone assumed someone in the area had lost or let their rabbits go and they had subsequently established a presence there. One spring morning, with feelings of guilt for abandoning a pet and with real hope that being with other rabbits would be better for him than being cooped up in solitary confinement, the family let Brownie go.

Brownie let the boy pet him once, then took off into the underbrush. Several days went by during which the boy prayed for Brownie every day. Once he saw Brownie on the edge of the yard, chewing grass. After that, none of the family ever saw him again.

Did Brownie become a meal for some wild animal? Is he happy being free in the wild? The young boy seems to have forgotten Brownie already, faithfully believing that things are well. His parents however still wonder, "Did we do the right thing? And what have we learned?"

All's well that ends well. When there is no clearly defined ending, however, we may choose to live in hope.

# 9 | LEFTY

*He* was a really cute kitten. Not more than eight weeks old and jet black. I could hear him purring even before I got into the exam room. That was surprising, as the reason the owners brought him in was because of a serious injury. They suspected a broken leg.

The poor little fellow really was in a lot of pain. A physical exam revealed a lot of bruising of the left hind leg as well as a fracture of the femur, the main leg bone that runs from hip to knee. Whenever I would touch the leg, no matter how gently, the kitten would cry in pain. His owner approved the use of painkillers and radiographs to determine the extent of his injury. Once the analgesic took effect we were able to manipulate the leg enough to get clear x-rays. Alas, the fracture was multiple, and a big bone chip had broken off and become detached. Fortunately the break was in the middle of the bone and did not affect either the hip or knee.

I explained to the owner that because the bony fragments were not close together we were unlikely to get good healing if the leg were splinted or cast. With the fracture site and the type of break however, the prognosis for healing with bone pinning and wiring was excellent.

We call the kitten Lefty now. Lefty, because his left hind leg now has wires and a pin in it. Lefty, because he was left behind. You see, when the owners heard the cost of orthopedic surgery they said they would take the cat home and shoot it. When we offered to put the kitten to sleep humanely at no charge, they were willing to allow that. But by then all of us in the clinic had already fallen in love with

Lefty. After a quick discussion we decided to try to find a way to get proper treatment for the brave little kitten, who had hardly stopped his purring since coming in the door. The owners were happy to sign over ownership of the kitten to us, so we might treat him if we could manage it.

Members of the clinic staff banded together and offered their time and finances. Together with donations from a few interested clients we raised the costs of surgery and follow-up care. Lefty came through surgery with flying colors and began using his leg as early as the next day.

Guess what? You bet—from the minute anesthesia wore off he was purring again. And he never stopped. He is now the proud owner of a new home, complete with more humane humans!

# 10 | A TIME FOR REFLECTION

*There* is a time to live, a time to die, a time for joy, and a time for tears.

It was our time for tears. We gathered around as a family and called our faithful dog Sultan over to us. He happily came to us, the only one without tears in his eyes. Even so, I think he somehow sensed that he was going to die. He licked each of us and lay down on the ground. A quick injection and a big sigh, and he passed away. We placed him on a blanket and wrapped him up, together with the favorite treat our daughter gave him and the favorite toy our son gave him. I took him away for cremation, gone from our lives but not from our hearts.

The suddenness of Sultan's sickness surprised us. He had always been happy and healthy except for the occasional ear infection, which we kept under control by regular ear cleaning. Then we began to notice over a few weeks that he had lost a little spunk. On physical exam, the color of his gums was just a touch dark, and there were a few red scabby areas on the skin that looked like an infection. Bacterial skin infections caught early are usually easily treatable. I started him on a course of antibiotics, and took samples of hair and skin for fungal culture to check if that was cause of his skin problem. After 10 days of treatment the skin was worse, while the fungal culture was negative. The next thing was to take a blood sample and skin biopsies. When those results came back the verdict was in and it was a sad one—Sultan's white blood cell level was more than ten times the normal level. They were cancerous, and it was the cancerous cells causing his skin problems. By this time the skin lesions had spread over his entire body. The technical name for his condition was Acute Lymphoblastic Leukemia. In everyday language that means a quickly developing cancer which has a poor prognosis, even with extensive treatment.

I remember setting off for the university immediately, to pick up drugs needed for chemotherapy. Then, wondering whether that was best, I turned around and headed back to the clinic. Then I turned around again after deciding the only fair thing was to give Sultan the most complete treatment available. Then I decided to wait until I had a chance to discuss it with my wife. Then I stopped on the side of the road and just felt anxious. I was gaining an appreciation of what some of my clients go through when faced with a serious diagnosis that gives their pet a poor prognosis for survival.

After a long discussion with my wife we decided to give Sultan medicine that would help him feel better but not to put him through the experience of chemotherapy. We did not want him to experience the serious side effects considering that most likely, even heavy duty chemotherapy would not cure the problem. So it was that after another three weeks or so, when he started to get worse again, we gathered as a family to end his suffering. His time for release, our time for tears.

Times of difficulty are often times when we are most open to learning, and so often the humblest of sources can teach the most. The frailty of life struck me, and the bond of loyalty between young children and a dog amazed me. Our daughter still keeps Sultan's name tag on her necklace. The faith of my four-year old son was an example to me—"It's okay, Daddy, don't cry. God gave Sultan for us to take care of for a while and now He will take care of Sultan in heaven and when we go there we can play with him again."

# DANGER ZONE

As a veterinarian I have had the privilege of working over-seas, in the Caribbean, Asia and the Middle East. People who have lived in "different" parts of the world know how things that happen there can be, well… different.

"So what do we do now?" I asked my interpreter, who looked as worried as I felt. "J..j..ust be c..c..c..calm!" he stammered. There were five of us, surrounded by a group of angry men, many of whom were brandishing machetes.

Things had started out nicely enough that morning. The long, tiring walk over rolling hills, through a surging river, deep valley, and dense vegetation was complete. Shouts of welcome greeted us upon our arrival at the remote Hai-tian village. We had brought along medicines and vaccines for local animals, and the villagers were happy to see us. They all seemed eager to bring their livestock and few pets for veterinary examination, deworming and vaccination against anthrax. Of the five workers in our group I was the only (and first that some children there had ever seen) white man. It was quite a sight to see wary children hiding behind trees, trying to get a peek at this new sort of pale ghostly person and yet not be seen themselves. A quick glance in their direction resulted in screams of excitement and a scattering of bodies. Some adults too were looking me over, but much more closely and less discreetly, with thinly disguised curiosity.

The idea of having visitors in the village was exciting enough that everyone living there showed up to watch the proceedings. As each person shyly led, dragged, or carried their animals over for evaluation, the atmosphere was light and jovial. I felt as if we were center ring in a popular circus. Laughter and knee-slapping hilarity reigned. I quite enjoyed evaluating and treating the pigs, donkeys, and dogs brought for examination. To be honest, the interest and attention given me, including numerous explorative touches to my blond head, was pretty fun too.

Problems started with the first cow. Our veterinary protocol included taking blood from all cattle, and this had been explained in advance to the village leaders. We were checking blood samples for presence of leptospirosis and brucellosis organisms, which cause disease that can have a significant impact on both animal and human health. In the eyes of the locals, however, taking blood from an animal was a whole lot more serious than administering vaccines or treatment for disease. Several years earlier, government officials had come through and tried to remove and kill every single pig as part of a disease eradication program on the island. Most of the owners had never received compensation and were, understandably, still furious about the whole episode. The minute we tried to get our first blood sample, that previously hidden anger and resentment sprang to the surface. The villagers suspected us of being government agents getting information on diseases that would lead to further animal slaughter. The hostility from our hosts was almost palpable; neither the machetes nor the yelling contributed to any sense of security. Readers familiar with Haitian history and culture know that we would not have been the first people there hurt by an angry and suspicious crowd. In this remote village, a days walk from civilization, we had little choice but to talk our way out of this tense predicament.

Fortunately, some men on our team originally came from that region of Haiti, and were able to appeal to the villagers for calm. Once we assured the people that we would not take any blood samples they put away their weapons and allowed us to continue vaccinations and medical treatments. We were able to finish our day's work—without blood samples but with quite a story to take home!

Many are the times I have administered treatments to a pet under the owner's watchful eye. But never have I felt myself under so much scrutiny, or quite so nervous, as in that small Haitian village one hot day in July!

# 12 COMMUNICATION

$\mathcal{I}$nternational disease control in animals has become quite important recently, with concern over the spread of diseases such as Avian Influenza, BSE (Bovine Spongiform Encephalopathy), West Nile Virus, and FMD (Foot and Mouth Disease). When I read news articles and stories of disease control I recall my days working in the Middle East.

I was working with a group of people who were purchasing sheep and goats from many different locations in order to bring them together into a large research center. In order to develop a breeding program that would yield statistically significant results, we needed over a thousand breeding animals. Each one had to pass a physical examination prior to purchase. There were a number of infectious diseases that concerned us, and we wanted to do what we could to prevent them. FMD was endemic (present in low levels all the time) and vaccination against that disease was routine. What we did not know, however, was how common other diseases were. Of particular interest was Brucellosis, a disease which people can contract from animals. To determine the prevalence of that disease, each animal had its blood tested after arrival at the research center. Our plan was to then formulate a control program, depending on the level of disease discovered. Such a control program could consist of quarantine, culling, vaccination or a combination of each. Surprisingly to us, out of the entire number of stock purchased, there was only one animal that tested positive for Brucellosis.

It was late at night when we discovered that positive case, a young female goat. I decided that the best course of action was to destroy the affected animal humanely, before it could spread the disease. Other than the night watchman, who offered to help me, all research center staff had left for the day. As I did not yet speak Arabic well I was unable to explain to him what I was doing. No doubt he suspected I was planning to administer some life-giving elixir, since he regarded me as a highly trained foreigner who was able to do amazing things for animals with the tools and medicines I had. He expertly held the goat still and tipped up its head as I carefully found the jugular vein. He whistled in amazement when he saw the blood freely flowing into the syringe that contained "medicine," which actually was the concentrated anesthetic that would humanely put the goat to sleep by stopping her heart. He carefully watched as I depressed the syringe plunger and injected the solution into the vein. As I stepped back, the goat lost consciousness and died. The watchman's eyes became as big as saucers while he stared open-mouthed from me to the goat and back again. Exactly what he was thinking I will never know but he made it clear to me he would tell no one what had happened that night.

It wasn't until much later that the irony of the whole situation struck me. There I was, a newly arrived animal healer trying to convince a trusting farm laborer that I actually intended to kill the goat and discard it—something unheard of in that region! Meanwhile, my kind but incredulous assistant was going to do his best to shield me from anyone finding out about what he thought must certainly have been a serious mistake.

That just goes to show—in veterinary research and practice as well for life in general, communication is the key. Good will towards each other is probably most essential, but speaking the same language helps a lot too!

# 13 | A LITTLE LIGHT

*There* she was, chewing her cud. Well, sort of. Her mouth was not closing all the way, she was acting as if it hurt to chew, and there was far more spillage from the mouth than usual. At least, as far as I could see. Tied to a pole in the small dark tin hut, she stood in stifling heat. Outside, the temperature was at least 50 degrees Celsius. It was often that hot in this Middle Eastern country, but inside the hut it was probably much hotter yet. And humid. A path worn deeply into the wet and dirty straw like a merry-go-round showed the extent of the cow's short chain. The farmer explained that her weight loss over the last two months made her look like a skeleton. He had no idea what the problem was, or what to do about it. Several weeks earlier the farmer had asked the local medicine man to come and have a look at the cow. The medicine man's diagnosis was distemper and his recommended treatment was several burns with a red-hot iron on each side of the cow's body.

That sounds strange to us in the western world, but such branding (known as *wassam* on the Arabian peninsula) was still commonly used for treatment of health problems both in people and animals. Many men there have burn spots at the base of their skulls, which was the treatment of choice for headache. Many more have scars on their abdomens from burns given them as babies for treatment of colic.

At any rate, the *wassam* did not have any effect on his cow, so the farmer asked for help from another animal care worker, who had some training in western medicine. This man had a look at the cow and diagnosed infection, for which his treatment was a series of tetracycline injections, the only antibiotic available to him. After some time it became clear that repeated injections were not making much of a difference either. It was at that point I happened to be visiting, so the farmer honored me by asking for my opinion.

Stepping into the oven of a hut I ran my hands over the cow's trembling body and could find nothing except the expected load of ticks. The emaciated bovine was moderately dehydrated and extremely stressed. I asked the farmer for a flashlight, and he ordered his teen-aged son to bring one. The boy told his younger brother, who yelled at his three-year old sister standing nearby, who ran to get a flashlight from her mother. In the meantime, the farmer asked me about what sort of blood test or other laboratory evaluation I could do to diagnose the problem. I replied that a thorough examination reveals the most information and only then can we tell if additional testing is worth doing. Although he thought my examination was done, I considered it barely started, as the lighting was so poor I could hardly make out the cow's eyes or mouth.

The mother had given a flashlight to the toddler who gave it to her older brother who tried to give it to me but was intercepted by the teen-aged son who gave it to his father who passed it to me. Holding the flashlight, I pried open the jaws and peered down into the cow's mouth. Her teeth looked worn but normal, the gum color was fine, and the tongue was fine...except for a reddened spot at the back on the left...and there I saw, rubbing against the tongue, a piece of plastic tubing. It had become wedged over the molars and was cutting into the gums causing irritation, inflammation, and infection. It also was preventing the cow from closing her mouth all the way.

Once I had obtained a pair of pliers (passed along family tree as the flashlight had been), I quickly removed the plastic pipe with only a little complaining from the cow. She immediately seemed more contented, and started eating right away. As they told me later, the cow completely recovered and even became pregnant few months after that!

This story illustrates three things that an experienced veterinarian once told me never to forget: common things are common, simple things are simple, and there are more things missed from not looking than from not knowing.

As for life in general, let's remember too—when we are walking around in the dark, a little light can make a big difference.

# PART 2

# MUNDANE AND MIRACULOUS

# 14 OUCH!

*Y*EOWWW! I could not believe the pain! Never before in my life have I experienced anything like it.

My name is Scooter. I come from a city but spend a lot of time at the country home of a friend of mine, Caesar. He is used to running around outside all day but I am not. I prefer lounging in the house and only barking if anyone has the audacity to bother me. Still, there are a lot of interesting things in Caesar's country yard. He and I go tearing around all over the place; chickens and cats and wild animals scurry out of our way in great panic—what fun!

One morning this summer, however, Caesar's owner went away and locked us indoors. Well, she thought she had. She only secured the screen door though, so when some new sort of pompous looking creature came waddling across the yard, Caesar and I both went absolutely ballistic. Caesar scratched through the door—it wasn't me, really! Once that flimsy screen was gone there was nothing holding us back. Strange thing is, that proud little prickler didn't run away like the rest of the animals we chase. He just stopped strolling along and turned to face us. We both headed straight for the stranger, barking furiously. Out of the corner of my eye, and too late to do the same, I saw Caesar (the traitor!) turn away at the last second. He obviously knew something that I did not. With great vigor and misplaced enthusiasm I clamped my jaw around the intruder, shook him violently, and tried to pin him to the ground.

Oh, what lightning bolts of pain shot to the center of my being from my nose and eyes and face! In a desperate attempt to push it away I thrust my paws against the body of my adversary. Then, oh what pain pierced my paws, too! In my haste to disentangle from this frightening experience I fell onto, then kicked at what was left of the enemy, leaving me with additional agony in my left shoulder and back leg as well.

How I managed to rid myself of the terrible beast I don't remember, but I couldn't open my eyes at all. Anytime I tried to do so the scratching on my eyeballs was unbearable. I couldn't close my mouth or even swallow because it hurt even worse when I moved my tongue or jaw. In fact, I could hardly even walk because it hurt to move my legs. So I just stood there with my head down, drooling. After what seemed like hours I heard a car come in the driveway and Caesar's owner returned home. When she came around the corner she screamed. That scared me too, because I didn't know what was going on and certainly couldn't help her. After a few minutes she calmed down, however, and carefully bundled me into the truck and off to the vet clinic.

There were a lot of "ooohs" and "aaahs" there too, from bystanders. More than that I do not remember, other than another prickly sensation in one front leg. Everything went black then. I must've passed out. When I woke up it was as if I had entered another world!! I felt a bit drugged, mind you, but there was almost no pain and I could move again! It felt so good just to be able to lick my nose! You can't imagine what pleasure that simple act gave me. And to swallow! And to see! My eyes were still sore but it wasn't so painful to blink or to move my eyes around. Although my legs were sore and I limped a bit at first, in only two days I felt great again. For some reason Caesar's owner kept on dropping liquid into my eyes for a week and forced hard round bitter things into my mouth for two weeks. They brought me back to the vet clinic several times too. But that is a fine place to visit as far as I'm concerned, because I usually get a treat there. I've seen some funny critters at the clinic too, like snakes and lizards (which I am not sure about), birds and even a rabbit (which I dearly wanted to chase).

As for Caesar (who only got stuck with four quills, while I had over 1200!), well, he is still my friend. Either we dogs have short memories or we forgive easily, because I still follow him around and we have lots of fun together. The whole experience at the veterinary clinic was good, too. I will happily go back again—unless I ever run into a porcupine there!

# 15 | UNLOVED

*My* name is Unloved. I am completely alone, huddled in a snow bank against a tree, wanting above all else to have a home. The northern lights are dancing, and the pain of my empty stomach is lessening as time goes by, even though I have had nothing to eat for days. The burning sensation in my ears and tail has also subsided, and I cannot feel them at all. Yesterday I saw a bird hit the power wire and fall to the ground. My killing instinct flared up when I saw it beating the snow in an ever-weakening vortex, but I had no strength to pounce. As I watched it die I felt a strange kinship that I had never known before.

My old name was Sammy. Almost a year ago my masters came and rescued me from the pound. Apparently the big masters got me for my little master, to celebrate new life at Christmas. I don't remember much from before that day, but I will never forget the way my little master's eyes glowed when he hugged me as if he would never let me go. His hug was so fierce that it almost hurt. I was the best, coolest, cutest, and most wonderful kitten he had ever seen, and the more praises he lavished on me, the more I purred.

Life was grand in my new home at first. My job was to sleep when no one was home, play like crazy whenever the opportunity came, and purr and rub against all the new friends I met. I fulfilled my duty with enthusiasm to the best of my ability, and was amply rewarded with attention. There was a lot of love, lots of food, many hugs, and glorious sleep.

In time, however, my masters became less interested in me. There was less time spent together and fewer introductions to friends. I experienced less and less love, and there were even forgotten meals. I noticed that there was less peace in the house too, with arguments about who was responsible for me. I didn't really mind who would take care of me. I wondered what I had done wrong to become less important than before. It seemed that the more I showed how much I needed to be with my masters, the less they wanted me. There were more harsh words and more anger, and finally the big masters started to threaten that they would bring me back to the pound. That really bothered my little master, who tried to keep me fed and watered but still didn't seem to value my friendship. Late one night after another fight and more threats he became so upset and scared that he snuck out and dropped me off, far away from the house. He loved me and wanted to set me free, he said. I could tell his motivation was love because he was crying just like the time he first saw me.

But I feel so miserable now. Since that night I have twisted my leg on a slippery branch, been chased by a dog, lashed by the wind, and punished by the cold. I've given up looking for my home. I feel exhausted...weary...

Have you ever noticed how the northern lights look like angels? Tonight there is a large black hole in that curtain of light – is it my Master's hand reaching down to cradle me? Suddenly I feel warmth and peace. Maybe there is new life for me at Christmas after all.

My new name is Hope...

# 16

# SMALL BUT IMPORTANT

$\mathcal{D}$on't laugh, but my name is Teacup. I am not very big—only 3.2 kg, which is not even seven pounds. Plus, I am only eight months old. But already I have been through more medical testing and procedures and seen more of the country than most dogs do in a lifetime. I was three months old when my owner bought me. She brought me to the vet a few times for health checks and vaccines. Back then I felt a bit funny already, but since I was kind of nervous in the clinic, it didn't show. At home sometimes, my thinking would get fuzzy, at times I would feel woozy and almost fall over, and my vision was sometimes blurred or completely gone. Time would stand still, and all of a sudden I would come to my senses and find myself standing motionless, with saliva trickling out of my mouth.

To be honest, although I did feel strange, I did not know something was seriously wrong. My owner did though, and brought me to my veterinarian several more times. At first, every time we went I acted just fine because my adrenaline was going and that masked any sign of health problems. I remember well my owner shaking her head on the way home and saying, "Teacup, what are we going to do with you? That man must think I am a nutcase because you always act fine at the clinic. But you are just not right—I know it!"

One time at the clinic they took my blood for analysis (I didn't even wince) and it was normal as well. On our way home that day my owner said, "Teacup, what are we going to do with <u>me</u>? Maybe I am imagining all these problems."

Several days later I started feeling worse and vomited a few times; when I went into the clinic I couldn't see a thing. I hardly remember that visit, but it included more blood samples and some other things like pictures of my insides or something. I had to spend the day there even. I remember it well because it was just about the only time I had gone for more than an hour or two without hearing my owner's heartbeat. I worried more about that than anything else I had experienced before. Unfortunately, things were to get worse.

The diagnosis they told my owner was something I never even knew existed—an "extra-hepatic porto-systemic shunt." That is, when my body was being formed in the womb there were blood vessels carrying blood around my liver (normal in fetal development) but after I was born, one of those vessels did not close down to force more blood through the liver. Since part of the liver's job is to filter metabolic poisons out of the blood, the levels of those poisons slowly got higher in my body. As my body grew bigger (yes, I was even smaller before!) the demands on my liver became greater and the level of poison higher. Hence my mental dullness and other problems.

Now that my vet knew what the problem was, it should be easy to fix, right? Wrong! My owner ended up having to take me to a university veterinary college where highly trained surgeons operate with sophisticated equipment. There were more blood tests than I can recall and then one morning they wheeled me into the surgical suite. It took more than five hours of surgery, including additional testing with dye injected into my blood stream and moving x-rays. Finally they found the abnormal blood vessel. The vet put a special metal and clay clip around it. Apparently, during the six weeks after surgery, the clay part of the clip slowly absorbed fluids and expanded so that the blood vessel became pinched off more and more over time. This process had to happen gradually, so that my body had a chance to develop new blood vessels through the liver.

Let me tell you, the surgery worked! I feel great! My zest for life has increased, my vitality is restored, and all worries are behind me. Now whenever I am scared I get a chance to jump up and listen to my best friend's heartbeat. I just love the cuddling. Her friends say I am developing characteristics just like her! I consider that a supreme compliment.

My owner had some big bills to pay. I don't know much about money but I do know she had to cash in some kind of pension fund to cover the cost of the surgery at the university. I understand money makes some people stressed and upset. It seems to make my owner happy though; she says it brought me back to life. She says I am a miracle, a gift. Well I know the truth and now you do too...she is the miracle, a gift to me.

# 17

# DISCORD IN PURR-LAND

*N*ot many people know it, but cat civilization began thousands of years ago in the cradle of the Tigris and Euphrates rivers. Back then all cats believed themselves to be the pinnacle of created beings, and most still do.

The territory which cats laid claim to as their own they called Purr-land, and all cats lived together in peace. Over a number of years the cat population grew and grew; some cats started traveling to new parts of the world. Isolated groups of cats developed their own distinct societies, languages and practices; one of the largest groups migrated to a region they called Meow-land.

Centuries went by and generations succeeded generations until most Purrers were blissfully unaware of the existence of Meowers, and vice versa. The Meowers and Purrers appearance even changed such that, over time, just by looking, they could tell each other apart. The two societies of cats became more distinct and other than a few individuals who interbred or did a lot of traveling, both groups of cats continued to live lives quite isolated from the other group.

The world became smaller and smaller though, as less land was available for cat development and travel became faster and less expensive. Over time, members of Meow-land society and those of Purr-land society became more and more aware of each other.

Unfortunately, this led to a collision of their worlds. Purrers felt superior to Meowers. This was obvious to them, as the cat gods clearly favored Purrers, evidenced by a wonderful habitat and an abundance of prey in their land. Meowers felt superior to Purrers. This was obvious to them, as the cat gods clearly favored Meowers, evidenced by their thriving in a harsh environment and the successful use of their god-given ability to find alternative sources of food.

Some cats felt equally at home in Purr-land and in Meow-land despite the differences of culture and environment. Most Purrers however, found it more comfortable to live in Purr-land because they faced less discrimination there. The same was true of most Meowers in Meow-land.

Meowers started to envy the natural resources of the Purrers, Purrers started to envy the material wealth of the Meowers, and both began to feel the need to protect their belongings from the others. Purrers resented Meowers muscling in on their source of prey, and Meowers resented Purrers getting the reward of Meowers' hard work. Finally the Purrers decided they had taken enough abuse and needed to do something about it. Their leaders researched the annals of a previous great world culture and found that dinosaurs had found themselves in a similar situation. The dinosaurs had elected to fight each other. Because that previous world power had faced almost identical problems to what the cats did now, and because the logic of the dinosaur arguments seemed sound, the Purrers decided to launch battle against their adversary, the Meowers.

It may seem hard to believe, but the small number of Meowers and Purrers who wanted to pursue peace and diplomacy and self-sacrifice were drowned out by cries of hatred. And the cat fur started to fly. This is why today many cats cannot get along and why we have sayings like "don't have a hissy-fit" and "spitting-mad" and "fighting like cats". Despite the fact that many cats still think they rule the world, in reality they do not. One can only imagine what could have been.

It's hard to understand that type of thinking and behavior because we are humans and everyone knows that people are superior to cats.

Humans would never act like that.

# 18 | HOMECOMING

*W*ow! Isn't life grand! I've just come home from padding around my new neighborhood, checking out the sights, sounds and especially the smells! Tires are an awesome collage and you don't have to go far for a whiff of cat. Some days when the breeze is right I swear I've smelled something wild. I followed that smell once before in my old neighborhood but ended up getting completely lost. I actually ended up being trapped, caught and picked up by a nice person who brought me to a really neat place with more dogs than I have ever seen together in one place before. Talk about smells! Now that was exciting!

Even more exciting was when I met my new master there. The thrill was so great that I made sure the whole place knew of my joy! Never before had my exuberant welcome of a new friend been met with as much excitement in response! My tail stayed attached to my hind end, and my newfound friend's wide grin didn't crack his cheeks, much to my surprise!

Anyway, to get to my point, the reason why I am so ecstatic and think that life is super is the fact that I feel accepted! Today I managed to dig out of the yard and went touring around my new neighborhood like I often did at my old place. You'll never guess what happened when I got back! I was getting close to home and slowed down to a cautious walk, afraid of the trouble I would be in, and not looking forward to derision and punishment. My tail was between my legs and my head hung low.

The reason for my worry is that in the past when I arrived home after wandering, I was bawled out, told I was a bad dog, and given a swat. You can imagine my confusion and distress when, happy to return home, angry words greeted me, with harsh tones and physical punishment. Why come home at all from a delightful barrage of sensual pleasure only to have it replaced with an onslaught of abuse that leads to emotional distress?! Well, that always used to be my lot.

Today, however, as I slunk into view of my new home, fearful of anticipated repercussions, I saw someone standing on the porch waiting. I just knew I was in for it big time. Sure enough, my master came running out towards me. I cringed and winced but instead of the expected blow I was received with joy! My master scooped me up in his arms, and hugged me! He stroked me and told me how much he loves me and how wonderful it was that I was home again.

Awesome!! Isn't life grand?! Now I am feeling part of a family again, loved and accepted instead of condemned.

You know, unless my master learns how to train me to stay home, I won't. I am eager to learn. I just can't do it by myself. As I said, it is my nature to wander—how I know it. But I can change. Today when I came home I experienced the only kind of love I know—unconditional, non-judgmental, and enthusiastic. The way my new master is, no matter where I wander I sure will look forward to coming HOME!

# 19 | MIRACLE

*D*o miracles really happen? Of course they do. Just ask Fenton.

Fenton was a typical young lad, full of zest for life and a lover of animals. Every kind of animal appealed to Fenton, and he often visited the library to look up information about one species or another. Of course, there was the constant appealing to his parents to PLEASE, PLEASE, PLEASE, let him have a pet. His parents would have loved to let him, as he was quite responsible and would no doubt benefit from the companionship of a four-legged friend. Unfortunately, they had found out at an early age that Fenton had allergies to animals.

These allergies were not the kind you just put up with. No, Fenton was rushed to a hospital emergency ward on several occasions because of extreme allergic reactions. He needed to carry drugs around with him for use in case of emergency. Even going into a house where a cat lived could be life threatening for Fenton because his airways would constrict and his lungs fill with fluid. Just walking past a caged bird could be trigger the reaction. Going to the zoo was too risky, and owning a pet was out of the question. Rather than having a pet to play with Fenton had to satisfy his desire with the poor substitute of looking at pictures, and owning goldfish. Fish were nice, but not enough for Fenton.

One day after school Fenton went over to the house of a new student to play. This boy had something he wanted to show Fenton—a hedgehog! Its quills, pointy nose, defense mechanism of snorting and its self-anointing behavior all thrilled Fenton. It wasn't until he got home and was telling his parents about the visit that it dawned on all of them at the same time—there was no allergic reaction from the hedgehog! None at all.

So it was that Fenton became the proud owner of Princess, a young female hedgehog. She was an awesome pet for Fenton; they were so gentle together that she never poked him, never acted afraid. The next four years were some of the best years of Fenton's life; a life filled with a sort of companionship he thought could never be his.

It came as a shock one day, when Fenton noticed Princess' food falling out of her mouth. On closer inspection, he realized that she had actually lost a lot of weight. Looking into her mouth, horror of horrors, he saw a drop of blood! Immediately Fenton alerted his mother, who phoned the vet clinic and headed out the door with Fenton and Princess.

At the clinic, after examining Princess, I did not have good news for Fenton. Inside Princess' mouth there was a growth that appeared cancerous. She also had a large burden of mites on her body. In addition, there were signs of a urinary tract infection. Very possibly, Princess' immune system was affected by cancer. Despite being treated for mites and taking medication for her urinary tract infection, Princess' long-term prognosis was poor indeed. Ideally, I would have liked to take biopsies of the affected tissue for analysis and surgically remove the growth. However, Fenton's mom said that would be too costly for them. It was with a heavy heart that I watched Fenton leave, even though he was committed to hope for the best and determined to faithfully give the medication.

A month later when Fenton came back with Princess he was not looking very happy, because he thought Princess would have to be put to sleep. Princess herself, however, was looking much happier than before! Her skin was less red and flakey, and it appeared that the urinary tract infection was under control. Most amazingly, inside her mouth there were hardly any signs of the tumor any more! There was a slight area of abnormally colored gums but none of the large protruding growth like before. Fenton was overjoyed, to say the least. We could not be sure Princess would be free from further trouble with the tumor. However, there also was nothing else for us to do but give her a much better prognosis than before, thereby giving Fenton a reason to rejoice!

To a cynic, this whole episode could look like an inconsequential improvement of a silly little animal that should not be a pet in the first place, with a condition that had probably been initially misdiagnosed. But to Fenton, Princess' new lease on life was a gift joyfully received. And to me, it was a poignant reminder that when I really open my eyes I can see again that the mundane and the miraculous are really one and the same.

# 20

# LIFESAVER

*I* ran into him on Whyte Avenue one day. I don't remember what it was that got us talking but most likely it was his cat. It's not often I see a street person with a pet, and I remember walking up to him and asking if he needed a hand with the cat. Funny isn't it, how a pet can be the reason to start a conversation between people who would otherwise walk past each other, personal worlds miles apart with no known intersection. Yes, there are other common interests, but it is often pets that draw people together. Though I thought I was doing him a favor that day, it turned out to be I who received a gift—the story of Eugene and his cat Humvee.

Eugene was not technically homeless, as he did have a rented room in a small, run-down apartment nearby. He was subsisting on a disability pension that gave him a total of $480.00 per month to get by. A head injury in the workplace had changed his personality and affected his memory. When the happy, stable life he knew had fallen apart he fell apart too, and ended up living on the street, using a postal box for his address. The monthly cheque was all that came in the mail anyway, besides the flyers that were of no use other than to help keep him warm. Life on the street was hard, and although there was camaraderie among street people Eugene found himself spiraling downward in mind and soul. He considered, and once attempted, suicide.

It was shortly after a stay in the hospital that he met Leo. Leo was a newcomer who spent his days on the street but went home to a rented room every night. Leo and Eugene got along well and it wasn't long before Leo introduced Eugene to his cat Humvee. There was an instant and almost magical bond formed between Humvee and Eugene. Leo could see something special there, so when he decided to move to the big city, he not only worked out a rental agreement with Eugene for his room but also gave him Humvee.

According to Eugene, that was when his life changed. Suddenly, he said, he had something to live for! He kept his living area cleaner than he ever had before, and started learning what he could about cat health and how best to take care of Humvee. He discovered his income was not enough to cover rent and food for both himself and the cat, so he prioritized things in such a way that Humvee was always fed first and best. Truth be told, he said, there were days when Eugene rather than Humvee had to get by on leftover food. So Eugene got himself a job cleaning up the back of a store, and now manages to scrounge enough cash together to make ends meet.

Eugene now does nothing without taking Humvee along, and Humvee is always purring and seems contented as can be. Eugene says that things are wonderful compared to before. Not only does he have someone dependent on him but, as he often proudly states, "There ain't many others here that can say they own a Humvee!"

My discussion with Eugene got me wondering—who was it that benefited more from the bond between them? Who was the rescued one?

# 21

# PROTECTOR

*S*ome of the things we take for granted every day are actually quite exceptional indeed. Take my neighbor's yard for example. When you walk up to it you won't notice anything unusual. If you climb through the fence however, suddenly an injured bird will appear from beside a small nest on the ground, dragging a broken wing and screaming in alarm. If you follow that bird some distance it might run farther and suddenly develop a broken leg too, writhing in pain on the ground. If you get closer still, a miraculous healing will take place and the bird will get up and fly away. But wander back too close to the nest from which the bird came, and it will come back, scream louder and maybe even attack you, dive-bombing your head.

Most people will recognize this activity as typical of a nesting killdeer. Yet, isn't it amazing? I must admit that when I first came across a killdeer nest I thought it a pretty poor idea to situate it in the middle of an open field, with no protection. Having said that, I myself found the camouflaged eggs very difficult to find. The activity of parent birds (who seem to take an equal share of the nesting duties) however seemed a pathetic ruse, having the effect of drawing me toward the nest rather than away from it. I could not imagine how this could be an effective way to deter predators. But I began to realize that each time my dog came with me past the nest she was lured quite effectively and chased the parent birds like crazy, never even thinking about the nest. It only dawned on me over time that, as in so many other cases, natural defense mechanisms are exquisitely suited for meeting the need.

Last year the nesting pair of birds in my neighbor's yard laid four eggs. As far as we could tell, three survived. The birds I thought of as "stupid" had averaged better than I have in many of my endeavors!

Nesting birds, doing what they do best—being birds! And we humans—we could do worse than to sit back, watch, and learn.

# 22 | CATFIGHT IN THE KITCHEN

*H*er voice was ecstatic on the phone. "Doctor, it's wonderful! Jerry is giving Tom a thrashing today and I'm thrilled! That is the best thing we've seen for months!" It was true. Strange as it may sound, the catfight between Tom and Jerry was indeed a good omen.

Mrs. Kitchner had found a litter of kittens outside on her acreage almost 12 years ago. There were seven kittens huddled together in the straw, with their mother nowhere to be seen. Four had already died, and a fifth one would also pass away despite two days of intensive care and surrogate mothering by Mrs. Kitchner. Despite great odds that none of the kittens would survive, two did. Whether it was sibling rivalry between two kittens that had a strong drive to survive, or whether both had a dominant nature, from the day that both could move around on their own, these kittens were at each others throats. Literally. It was as though they had a love-hate relationship, with mutual grooming and purring one minute and what appeared to be vicious fighting the next. There never was any serious injury but it always looked as both were intent on killing the other. Tom and Jerry became the obvious names picked by Mrs. Kitchner, who initially tried to play the referee but who soon realized there was no point in trying to intervene. It usually was Tom who instigated the fighting but Jerry who appeared to be the victor. Why Tom kept on at Jerry we could never figure out, but it was a part of their lives for years.

When Tom and Jerry were 11 years old Mrs. Kitchner brought them in for an examination. She was not sure what was the matter, but she was quite sure that Tom was sick. Though it embarrassed her to say so, the reason she thought something was wrong was because Tom was not attacking Jerry any more. Starting about a month earlier, the two cats still played together but this playing never escalated into the battle royale that Mrs. Kitchner was used to seeing. Both cats seemed more quiet than usual. Though she was not sure which it was, one cat had to be eating less because there was more food left over than usual. Since Tom was the agitator in most cases, Mrs. Kitchner felt he must be ill. After physical exams and some lab testing however, we discovered that Tom appeared to be quite well but it was actually Jerry who was ill; he had a mass in his abdomen that was most likely cancerous. During an exploratory surgery I removed a large growth from the intestine that had been almost completely blocking passage of intestinal contents. Jerry recovered from surgery well but the laboratory diagnosis of lymphosarcoma (a kind of cancer) gave a grave long-term prognosis. Jerry went home for recuperation and we discussed options of chemotherapy with Mrs. Kitchner.

By that time we had come to the realization that most likely, Tom had somehow sensed that Jerry was ill before we did, and that was probably why he stopped pestering him. Mrs. Kitchner resigned herself to life being different from before, and it only then struck her how much she had come to enjoy the strange relationship the two cats shared.

In time we decided that a course of chemotherapy would be Jerry's best chance for long-term survival. He had recovered fully from surgery and his physical state and blood results suggested he would be able to handle the additional therapy. He went through five rounds of chemotherapy and after the last round we decided that he should not get more. Though we would not know for sure until later whether the treatment was successful, we had done all we could for Jerry.

It was five days later that Mrs. Kitchner phoned with the good news. I had to agree. Although I have no idea how some pets have the uncanny ability to sense things that even our best lab testing cannot, Tom was telling us that Jerry was going to be a survivor. It was a week later that Jerry laid the next thumping on Tom when Tom attacked him—and the catfights continue, much to our delight.

# 23 | PRICELESS

*Ah*, the lowly hedgehog. If you've never known one, the thought of having one might seem a little strange. I mean they are usually asleep during the day and active at night, right? Besides, they aren't very cuddly, are they? And their natural diet consists mostly of slugs and bugs—yuck! Who would want one of them?

Well, that brings up the question of what gives an animal value. I don't mean their intrinsic value, because that is a big issue with philosophical and religious implications far too complicated to resolve in a short story. What gives a pet value to its owners/caretakers?

Let me tell you a tale of two hedgehogs. We'll call the first Rose. A teenager took Rose home from school from a friend who had brought the hedgehog to class. The friend decided to give her away because Rose had a scab on her nose that was not healing. In her new home, Rose did quite well for a while. After a few weeks, however, her new owners became aware that something was wrong because she was losing quills and not moving much. When I saw Rose at the clinic she was severely overweight, had an extremely large number of mites on her body, and also a respiratory infection. Fortunately, those problems could all be dealt with fairly easily. Unfortunately, the owners were not interested in providing the necessary care. They left the clinic hoping they could bring Rose back to school and that someone else would take her.

Then there is Prince. Prince was owned and cared for from the time of birth. He had been kicked out of his mother's nest at one day of age; we don't know why his mother abandoned him. From that first day the owners did the best they could to take over the functions of his mother, starting by feeding milk replacer, drop by drop every two hours. This saved his life, for baby hedgehogs weigh only a few grams, and are born deaf, bald and blind. His owners researched proper hedgehog management and then provided appropriate housing and food for years.

It seems that Prince grew up thinking he was a human, because he is as gentle as can be and never raises his quills. He answers to his name, has a daily routine that involves stops at various locations in the house, as regular as clockwork, and he loves being held and petted. The reason I saw him was that he had developed a health problem that was genetic in origin. Despite his owners' willingness to do everything possible, the problem was incurable and Prince would have to live with the condition. Prince's owners left the clinic intent on keeping him comfortable, seeking to maintain his quality of life as best possible despite the illness.

Which of these two pets, Rose or Prince, is more valuable? To put another spin on it—which owners do you think feel more enriched by their pet? In neither case was there medical intervention, yet the level of tender loving care was worlds apart.

Hedgehogs can illustrate the principle quite well: it is in giving that we receive.

# 24 | HINDSIGHT

$\mathscr{D}$aytona Randolph knows what it is like. The way a little nagging concern can grow into a disturbing worry, how worry changes into a fear that can grow until it borders on panic. What it feels like when, despite a willingness to do whatever you can, the situation is not in your hands, and you know it—big time.

You see, Daytona had a friend named Perky. And Perky was the best dog a person could have. Perky had a great nature and was fun to be with and had hardly any bad habits other than a tendency to eat unusual objects. That condition is called "pica" which is a funny sort of word but it wasn't funny for Perky, because she would end up vomiting and sometimes get diarrhea as a result.

So it was not that unusual that Perky got an upset stomach after eating a new sort of treat. Daytona and his parents expected her to get better on her own like before. When she was still vomiting a couple of days later, they took her to me to find out what the problem was. I was very concerned right away because there were signs of blood loss, liver failure and dehydration—this was no simple upset stomach! We took x-rays and a blood sample and found evidence of coins in the stomach and severe heavy metal poisoning. Unfortunately, despite intensive therapy and removal of coins, the damage to Perky's liver, pancreas, and kidneys was so severe that she passed away.

Daytona knows what it is like. The questions that come with the loss of a pet, the "why?" and "if only..." and "what if..." that cling to and irritate the memory like burrs that cannot be brushed off. What good can come of a disappointment like that?

One way to make sure something good comes from Perky's experience and loss is to share with you some of the lessons that Daytona learned. Preventing even one pet or child from a similar toxic reaction is what he wants to do. Most of all, he wants you to realize how coins can be very toxic. Before 1995, Canadian pennies were made of copper and although swallowing large numbers of them could cause illness, a few would not likely cause harm. After 1995, however, the mint started to make pennies out of a copper coated zinc alloy (US pennies are the same type of alloy). When stomach acids break down the copper coating, the more poisonous zinc is exposed. This can lead to the sort of problems Perky had.

Most folks still think that swallowing a few coins will not cause a problem. Perky, however, weighed over thirty pounds, and the toxins that killed her came from only five pennies. So please, remember Daytona's health advisory: keep all coins and especially pennies out of the reach of pets and little children.

Happily for Daytona, the story does not end with the loss of Perky. For Daytona also knows the joy of getting a new pet and how Buster (his new young pup) can help ease the pain of loss, even while it cannot replace the lost one. Buster is a healthy puppy and is fitting in well with the family. On top of that, Daytona entered a draw at the vet clinic and won a huge pet bed for Buster! And the pup loves it!

Remembering how he had to leave Perky in the past, what a different feeling it was for Daytona to walk out of the clinic with a healthy bouncy Buster and his new bed!

Amazing, isn't it—how even a lowly animal is used to bring laughter from mourning and joy from tears.

Daytona knows.

# 25 | LOVE ON A WING

*M*rs. Sweater was a fighter. So was her bird JPS. JPS, named after Mrs. Sweater's favorite bandmaster John Philip Sousa, was a cockatiel that had lived more than the expected 10-15 years. This was in spite of a serious deformity he was born with, a deformity that did not allow him to walk normally. In fact, none of his toes worked properly, leaving them useless, gnarled appendages that only got in his way. Because of his poor feet, he dared not fly either, because he could not land smoothly and would inevitably go head over tail feathers when he did.

Despite his handicap, the crippled JPS lived quite a life. Mrs. Sweater's husband, prior to passing away from emphysema, had given him to her. He had known that his wife always wanted a bird but as he was allergic to them, they could never have one in the house while he was alive. Just a couple of weeks prior to his passing (on the day Mr. Sweater was to be admitted into the palliative care unit), he went out and purchased a little bird. It was a baby cockatiel, Mrs. Sweater's favorite kind.

Unbeknownst to him, Mr. Sweater had the fleece pulled over his eyes. He paid a good dollar for the juvenile JPS but as he did not physically check him before leaving, the seller sent him away with a crippled rather than a healthy bird. Little did he know that the poor little bird's chances of survival were almost zero. He never did find out either, because Mrs. Sweater, who right away saw the deformity, never told him. Rather, she threw herself completely into ensuring the survival of the tiny avian, while at the same time taking care of her husband in hospital. During the first few weeks of JPS' life (which were the last few weeks of her husband's life) Mrs.

Sweater was run ragged, feeding her new baby bird by hand every hour and doing her best to make sure the crippled legs were not damaged by it's bedding. Handling the bird so much forged a bond between them, a bond reinforced by countless hours spent together after Mr. Sweater died. JPS and Mrs. Sweater were never seen without each other. Mrs. Sweater rigged up a little carrying pouch in which JPS rode around. She even got him to the point where he would climb out of the pouch to pass stool, and do so only on a certain cloth she carried with her all the time.

When I first met the two of them it was because JPS was having trouble with his eyes. They were red, swollen, irritated and watering a lot. Unfortunately the underlying problem was more severe. He had a corneal ulcer on one eye, secondary to sinusitis, an infection of the sinuses in his head. When birds get this sort of infection it can be very difficult to treat, and can cause bulging of the eyes like JPS had. We started treating him with oral antibiotics and eye drops and, although he never did recover completely, JPS did quite well for four more years. The relationship between the woman and bird was so special. It almost defied explanation, but everyone who met them had to conclude they were able to communicate together by some sixth sense. JPS, the cockatiel who would have been dead without Mrs. Sweater, seemed to thrive whenever he was close enough to hear her heart beat. Mrs. Sweater, who had nurtured and cared for him in a self-sacrificial way, said she always received much more from JPS than she had given. Both were so happy together.

It was a sad day when, just after his 19$^{th}$ birthday, Mrs. Sweater brought JPS because of new health problems. His stool had been getting loose, he was drinking more water than before, and his feet were swollen. He had developed kidney disease and gout, a condition dreaded by bird fanciers because of its grave prognosis. Although she did keep JPS another couple of weeks, he was losing weight and obviously in pain and it wasn't long before she decided it would be kinder to put him to sleep. We did so quickly and gently, and JPS was gone.

Through her tears, Mrs. Sweater was reminiscing. Her remembering would continue for years, but the overall emotion was one of gratitude. Thinking about how her husband had lovingly yet unwittingly brought home a young fledgling that was facing imminent death, she told me, "They meant it for evil, doctor, but God meant it for good!"

There is more to this story. Mrs. Sweater was living in a condominium unit that had passed a resolution to allow no new pets. There was, however, a grandfather clause that allowed tenants who already had pets to keep them. JPS was such an important part of Mrs. Sweater's life that she could not bear to be without him. Although JPS was irreplaceable, Mrs. Sweater did get another young bird and brought him in to her condo. She got another cockatiel that looked just like JPS, and no one but she could tell the difference!

# WHO'S FIRST?

Harry was a fit senior citizen who always looked after himself well. He never really thought much about his health, but like many of us simply took it for granted. His regular exercise was to go for good long walks with his best friend George Coulter. This he did on a daily basis, without exception. He watched his diet carefully and ate only food known to be good for him. Well, there were the occasional splurges, but not such that anyone would say he was compulsive. His personality was quite laid back and certainly not the type that would predispose him to heart or stroke problems. Overall, life was good for Harry. He had not much stress, enjoyed life a lot, and was always energetic and enthusiastic.

Then one year during Advent, while Harry's household was preparing for Christmas, he suddenly became quite depressed. He didn't feel like going on his walks, and eating did not hold the same appeal as usual. Over a two-day period Harry went from bad to worse. He was still happy but not energetic. His attitude was still enthusiastic but he did not have the strength to show it. He could feel that something was wrong but, as always, he took life as it came. He had the uncanny ability to simply accept things as they were, while at the same time hoping for something better.

When George saw that Harry was disinterested in going out with him he thought maybe Harry had just overdone it one evening and was very tired. By the third day of this kind of behavior however, George knew something serious was going on. Harry never much liked going to see the doctor but George decided to take him for a check-up, whether he wanted to or not.

When I saw Harry he was looking very lethargic indeed, not even wagging his tail when I petted him. A physical exam revealed he had serious problems. After a blood screen and a few other tests we concluded that he had an autoimmune disease where his immune system was attacking and destroying his own red blood cells. As a result of that he had severe anemia. Because of the lack of oxygen carrying capacity in his blood Harry's heart had to work very hard, yet was unable to keep up with oxygenation demands of his body.

Mr. Coulter realized that Harry's prognosis was poor, yet he wanted to do everything possible for him. Despite intensive therapy however, Harry became worse. Although we were giving him all recommended treatments it looked as if nothing was going to help him. Late one night, about 11:00 p.m., we sat next to Harry while I was giving him a blood transfusion. Mr. Coulter remarked, "You know doc, I've set aside twelve thousand dollars in a special 'Harry account' to allow us to spend as much as it takes to get him better."

"George," I gently replied, "if I could spend that money for you and have Harry healthy again, you know I would. But money is not the problem right now; there are certain things that money can't buy."

Poor George. Sobs racked his body as he cried, "I know. I know. How I wish it were different right now! I had hoped Harry would at least make it to Christmas. I can't buy peace or joy either and without this little guy around there won't be much of those for me this season. My only hope now is that things will be better for him when he passes on. Do dogs go to heaven, doc?"

"At Christmas time we remember Jesus birth, George. Isaiah foretold it when he promised that a virgin would give birth and the Son she bore would be called 'Immanuel,' meaning 'God with us.' Isaiah is also the prophet who foresaw of a time when peace would reign forever. His vision of the future has lions lying down with lambs, and cows eating together with bears. If all those other animals can be in heaven I sure don't see a reason why Harry couldn't be having a ball there with them, do you?"

But George wasn't listening, for just at that moment we both realized Harry had passed away. I left George alone with his beloved pet for a few moments, and then he got up to go. On the way out George turned back to Harry and said, "Hope to see you again, buddy! I'm still waiting for Christmas, and you're there already!"

# PART 3
# PETS ARE GREAT

# 27 | POINTERS FOR PET OWNERS

*P*ets are great! But they are not for everyone.

On the other hand, with a such a great variety of animals available and many pets looking for a loving home, it makes good sense to seriously consider the contribution an animal friend could make in your life, and you in its. Humans have always valued animals, from the herding sheep dog to the puppy playing with a small child to the old parrot sitting on a sailor's shoulder. Work, play, and companionship—all offered unconditionally to the person who befriends and takes care of one of God's lesser creatures.

When I was in grade three I desperately desired to own and care for an elephant. It certainly would not be any problem, I assured my parents, who for some reason did not agree. Elephants probably would not qualify as the most likely pet of the year for someone in urban North America, but have you ever thought of making room for a veiled chameleon? Or a pair of lovebirds? How about a ferret or an African hedgehog? Then there are chinchillas, hamsters, gerbils, and a host of other interesting and fun "pocket pets." Caring for pets offers a world of learning for children of all ages. Most of us have fond memories of some interaction with a dog, cat or other pet.

My advice to anyone thinking of getting a pet is basic: Be sure you have what it takes to make the relationship with your pet a good, long lasting, and healthy one. The most important requirements are an awareness of the needs of your selected pet and the commitment to meet them. Some pets will take more time than others, some take more space than others, some require a higher financial outlay, and some are more able to steal your heart. Be sure you know what is involved and are committed and prepared to meet your pet's needs.

The key to successful pet rearing is to tailor the housing, feeding, and level of socialization to your pet's needs rather than your own. Attempt to match the pet's natural environment as closely as possible. Be aware that if you take on a boa, the time spent socializing will be quite different than if you are caring for a blue-point Siamese! If you think the diet required by a tegu is gross, maybe you need to consider a terrier. The commitment to give a macaw a home will be much longer lasting than one made to a mouse. If you can't create an environment in which a water dragon would feel at home, think about fresh water fish. If you are the type that sleeps all day and are up all night, consider a sugar glider—you keep the same schedule!

In the following chapters we will look at several different types of pets and consider some of their advantages and disadvantages, and go over some pointers as to proper care. Hopefully the thoughts expressed here will lead to a greater appreciation of the wonderful variety of animal life we can experience, and result in happier, healthier pets!

# 28

# BIRDS

*B*irds are great! But they're not for everyone.

On the other hand, numerous types of birds are kept as pets, from the common finch and budgie to the exotic parrot, and other birds. The various types of birds have different living and feeding requirements; get information on the sort you are thinking of, to be sure you can supply its needs.

The size of living area required for each bird depends on its size and activity level. Ideally, an aviary should have sufficient area for flying as well as nesting, bathing, sunning and preening. Most pet birds kept inside a home may be suitably housed in an appropriate size cage with metal or plastic bars. Some larger birds do well on a bird stand. In any case, bird housing should have a removable floor (preferably covered with newspaper) for easy cleaning. The best perches are those most like what a bird would sit on in its natural environment, so why not use branches?! Cut them to size and secure them in a cage with leather thongs. These branches are not only easy to keep clean (simply replace the old branch) but are helpful with exercising legs and feet. Wooden perches require a thorough cleaning every few weeks as they can serve as a source of bacterial contamination. Since they are difficult to clean properly, consider plastic perches if you can't use the natural product. Sandpaper easily irritates and damages sensitive bird feet—please avoid such unnecessarily rough perching surfaces.

Food and water dishes should be plastic, metal or ceramic and easy to remove for cleaning. Daily cleaning of dishes prior to filling them with fresh food and water is recommended. Disinfection of dishes should be carried out weekly, along with cleaning of the cage floor. Non-metal dishes may be soaked in dilute chlorine bleach and rinsed off thoroughly before use. Washing in an automatic dishwasher will clean well and help with disinfection because of the high water temperature.

Most birds have toenails and beaks that grow continuously and need trimming periodically. Provision of a cuttle bone for birds to keep their beak in shape may lengthen time between beak trims. Having your bird's wings clipped is a simple and painless procedure which could prevent serious injury if it should escape from the cage or from your hand. Your friendly bird veterinarian can do the clipping and can also teach you the method for home use.

Commercial bird food is available for most birds, but can be deficient in minerals and/or vitamins, which degenerate over time. Always check for "best before" dates on food boxes and bags, or purchase bulk food from a bird supply store with good food turnover. Supplementing the diet with an avian vitamin/mineral mix will help prevent deficiencies; supplements are available in powder or fluid form. Generally, liquid supplements mixed with drinking water are easiest to give. Follow dosage instructions carefully. Added fresh fruit or vegetables are healthy treats for caged birds, but use seeds sparingly. All birds benefit from exposure to sunlight or a UV sunlamp for several hours daily, ideally about 12 hours per day. However, pet birds should never be taken outside to fly for exercise. Some birds may be allowed to fly loose inside but only be under strict supervision. Hazards such as mirrors, windows, electric cords, poisonous plants, chemicals, jewelry, stoves, ceiling fans, other pets, and toilets are present in every house. Ensure that you maintain optimal environmental temperatures—most pet birds do best with supplemental heat.

By the time a bird begins to show signs of disease it is usually very ill. If you see unusual discharge from eyes or nose, swelling anywhere on the body, sneezing, bleeding, or even if your bird just fluffs itself up and has reduced activity, food and water intake, get veterinary care for your bird as soon as possible. When you bring your bird in for an exam, bring the soiled cage flooring with you, as bird droppings can be a useful indicator of health.

# 29

# CATS

*C*ats are great! But they're not for everyone.

On the other hand, what a wide variety of breeds and types to choose from! Long hair and short tailed, short hair and long tailed, and anything in between. Beautiful expensive cats and beautiful other cats longing to be adopted and looked after. Breeding background determines the characteristics of cats to some degree, but the best word to describe the nature of cats is "variable." In general, however, cats tend to like a certain environment or way of life once they are used to it, and prefer to keep major life changes to a minimum.

People keep cats for numerous reasons, and since cats often live as long as 20 or more years given proper care, they can become an important part of the family for a long time. Cats need a quiet warm place to sleep, and a good quality diet. I recommend hard food over soft to make up the major portion of food intake in most cases. This helps prevent tartar build-up and gum disease, which is common in older cats who have not experienced routine dental care. Teeth brushing is an essential component of home dental care, and use of a medicated mouthwash is beneficial. Unless a cat is overweight or has certain health problems, free choice feeding is appropriate. Be sure to let the cat empty the bowl periodically, so that the old food does not build up on the bottom. Of course, fresh water needs to be available (free choice) at all times.

Hair coats of cats vary tremendously in thickness, length, and amount of shedding, depending on breed, climate, diet, and other factors. Be prepared for at least some shedding. And be willing, especially with long haired cats, to spend some time each day grooming so as to prevent hair mats, which can be very irritating and may lead to skin infections.

Cats are susceptible to a number of illnesses, just like the rest of us. The very young and very old are more likely to run into health problems, but fortunately the most common infectious diseases are mostly preventable by vaccination. Vaccination recommendations vary depending on lifestyle and amount of contact with other cats. Your veterinarian can advise you as to which vaccinations are most important in your cat's situation.

One common problem seen in cats is that of mineral deposits in the bladder. Especially in male cats but also in females, this can lead to a life-threatening blockage of the urinary tract. Fortunately, feeding a high quality diet is often sufficient to prevent this problem. However, if your cat experiences pain when passing urine, or if there is any sign of blood in the urine, arrange an appointment to get it checked out right away.

Another common problem, especially in longer haired cats, is hairballs—an accumulation of hair fibers in the cat's stomach. Usually cats vomit hairballs up and they cause no severe illness, but they can cause intestinal blockage. There are products specifically formulated to prevent hairballs and, if there is a buildup of hair in the stomach, to assist cats in vomiting it up; giving hairball control diets can also help.

Ideally, all cats kept as pets are neutered—the males castrated and females spayed. Not only does this help with population control, it also helps lessen certain behavioral problems and reduces the chance of hormone related cancers developing.

Cats are very popular as pets, partly because they can be relatively undemanding (sometimes). As with all pets, proper care and feeding, along with annual veterinary check-ups and vaccinations all work together to provide your cat the best chance for a long, healthy, and happy life.

# 30 | DOGS

$\mathcal{D}$ogs are great! But they're not for everyone.

On the other hand, there is a wide variety of types and sizes of dog, each with its own characteristics. Anyone willing to make a commitment to having a dog as a pet is almost guaranteed to find one that will be just right. Deciding what kind of dog to get is very important, and you should take careful consideration of what expectations you will have of your dog and your dog will have of you! One important point to make is that individual variation in personality of dogs within a breed can be as wide as that seen between breeds. Oftentimes crossbred dogs have wonderful temperaments and make ideal pets.

You can teach an old dog new tricks, but the best time to begin training a dog is when it is six to eight weeks old. Make training time fun and use praise as reward for desired behavior rather than punishment for poor behavior. In this short chapter we cannot cover all aspects of training but your veterinarian or local dog trainer can give you more information. Suffice it to say that although teaching your dog will require time, diligence and patience, your efforts will be rewarded when you train properly. A well mannered, affectionate and trustworthy dog is a joy to have around, and a lot easier to handle than a disobedient obnoxious rascal.

The keys to a healthy long life for your dog are proper care and feeding, combined with regular exercise, annual health check-ups, and vaccinations. There are a host of brands and types of food available; I recommend that you feed only high quality commercial dog food as the main diet. There are excellent biscuits that help control tartar, and a number of chewable toys are also designed to promote dental health. By the way, dental disease and obesity are two of the most common health problems I encounter in my patients. Do get specific advice on feeding your particular dog; do not forget that the adage "you are what you eat" is just as true for your dog as for yourself—don't skimp on food quality!

Many of the common infectious diseases of dogs are preventable by vaccination, and several other common conditions are treatable with medications. Recommendations for vaccination and other preventative medications depend on a dog's geographical location, lifestyle, and travel plans so I recommend that you discuss with your local veterinarian what would be optimal for your dog.

Sometimes, despite the best care you can give your pet, he or she may become ill. Signs of illness that require immediate attention include repeated coughing or vomiting, any vomiting of blood, no drinking for an entire day or no eating for two days, watery diarrhea that continues for more than two days, or any bowel movement with blood or black, tarry substance in it. Sometimes the only outward sign of illness we see is lethargy or depression, and a general disinterest in life. As with people, disease is often more severe in the very young and very old; if you ever have concerns about your dog's health please phone your veterinarian for advice on what to do.

Once you decide on a dog for you and your family, you are entering an adventure and learning experience. Almost all owners who willingly accept the commitment required in terms of time, food, and health costs insist that the return in the form of a dog's loyalty, commitment, and desire to please far outweigh their investment.

# 31

# FERRETS

*F*errets are great! But they're not for everyone.

On the other hand, what fun, inquisitive, personable characters they are! Although related to the mink and badger, ferrets are not wild animals but have been domesticated for thousands of years. They can make delightful pets as they generally get along well with people and are usually playful and intelligent.

Despite their gentle nature, ferrets are curious and quick. They can squeeze into very small spaces and love to explore unknown areas. That makes a challenge for owners, who should "ferret-proof" living areas and be sure there are no holes or openings wider than one inch through which an active ferret might escape. Favorite hiding places include piles of laundry, winter coats (check the sleeves), and dark corners under furniture (reclining chairs can be fatal for ferrets sleeping underneath). Many a missing ferret has been found inside a stove, fridge, or clothes dryer, having slipped in unnoticed while the door was open.

Ferrets are meat-eaters whose natural diet consists of killed prey. Fortunately, their nutritional requirements are similar to those of growing kittens, so the feeding of ferrets is relatively straightforward—high quality commercial kitten food made with animal source protein can meet normal nutritional requirements. There are also commercial ferret foods available, formulated for different age requirements. Hard food is better than soft food in prevention of teeth problems, and ensure the food is sufficiently concentrated to meet energy requirements. Treats in the form of cooked meat scraps may be given in moderation. Ferret owners all know how much of a sweet tooth they can have. Giving ferrets sweet nutritional paste supplements will often make them forget everything else. Moderation is the key. As with other pets, fresh food should used, and clean fresh water always be available.

A cat size cage with towels for burrowing makes a good bed for ferrets to sleep in and helps with control when it is inadvisable to let them have free run of the house. Most ferret kennels have hammocks in which ferrets love to lie. Never leave rubber toys lying around, as ferrets like to chew and have been known to swallow bits of rubber which can subsequently cause a blockage in the digestive system. Once I had to surgically remove a piece of carrot that was swallowed whole and got stuck in the intestine. I call him the "carrot ferret."

Ferrets are not only very sensitive to dog distemper, but can also contract other dog and cat diseases, including rabies. They also can catch (and spread) the human influenza or "flu" virus. Fortunately, most serious diseases can be prevented by vaccination. Other conditions, including urinary disease, skin infections and parasite infestations, are generally treatable. Unfortunately, several types of cancer are quite common among ferrets and are sometimes not curable. Unspayed females often have extended heat periods of up to five months, leading to bone marrow suppression and serious illness. That is why it is very important that non-breeding females be spayed. Spaying females and neutering males helps to reduce the natural ferret odor, but many owners also have their ferrets de-scented to prevent further objectionable odors being emitted from the scent glands near the anus. Most vendors sell ferrets already spayed or neutered and descented.

Once you choose to purchase a ferret, bring it in for a veterinary health exam and vaccinations. Then look forward to a fun and enlivening experience as you enjoy getting to know your unique new friend.

# 32

# HEDGEHOGS

*H*edgehogs are great! But they're not for everyone.

On the other hand, you must admit that they are cute. Perhaps that is why hedgehogs have become popular. Perhaps it is just that in our fast-paced society where we are gone most of the day and often home only at night, a nocturnal pet just fits in better sometimes!

In the wild, hedgehogs of various types are found in Europe, Asia, and Africa. People in the United Kingdom know hedgehogs as a fairly common garden inhabitant. Although there are a number of different species of hedgehogs, the two most popular types for pets are the European and African ones. In Canada I see the African variety much more commonly. Both types look more or less the same, but the African hedgehogs usually grow to not much more than a pound—half the weight of the European species.

In trying to create an environment in which a hedgehog will thrive, there are several points to remember. First of all, they are nocturnal, which means they are awake at night and sleep during the day. Secondly, they tend to be solitary in nature and are often easily frightened; underbrush or rocks make favorite hiding places. Thirdly, their preferred diet is mostly slugs and bugs—insects, worms, and the like.

Generally I suggest that hedgehogs be housed individually although if enough space is available, they can be kept in groups (fighting may be a problem). A large smooth-walled container such as a terrarium with a wire top can make a good home, with shredded newspaper (cleaned regularly) for bedding, some rocks and branches for hiding in, and a temperature maintained around 25 degrees Celsius. At ambient temperature lower than 18 degrees, hedgehogs may hibernate. So watch the temperature, especially in winter. Hibernation in captivity can be harmful. Most hedgehog owners have been told in the past to feed good quality kitten food as the main diet. It will do in a pinch, but hedgehogs are not cats; a diet of slugs and bugs is the best. So get out your spade and net and start collecting! Some people take their hedgehogs into the garden and let them find their own food. That is fine when the weather will allow it, but they can be very quick, so realize that you are taking a chance if you do that. Some pet shops carry commercial hedgehog food, and although these diets are generally not proven, they are helpful. Of course fresh water must be available at all times, and in general, food can be offered free choice. Recently I have seen a higher number of obese hedgehogs. Presumably overweight hedgehogs are more susceptible to heart and joint problems, like the rest of us.

If kept in a clean and appropriate environment, hedgehogs usually maintain good health, and live to about six or eight years. Some of the most common health problems I see include skin mites, respiratory infections, and internal parasites. These parasites can usually be diagnosed during routine health and stool exams, so bring your friend in for a visit to a veterinary clinic that deals with hedgehogs.

The biggest problem we have in examining hedgehogs is their tendency to roll up when frightened. About one-third of my hedgehog patients require anesthesia for a thorough exam. Although that is not very risky in healthy patients, it does increase cost and time associated with an exam. We often have the owner come right in and observe the process—someone told me recently it was the first time she had seen her hedgehog's belly!!

Only the gentlest and quietest of hedgehogs are safe with children because when frightened, the rolling up or jumping can cause minor quill injuries to hands. Probably one of the biggest hazards to a pet hedgehog is that of being dropped. I do not suggest hedgehogs as pets for young children.

As with other pets, hedgehogs carry some diseases that can spread to humans. Please remember to wash your hands after handling the hedgehog! Preventative measures are always better than having to cure a problem. So once you have found the hedgehog for you, bring him or her in for an exam and get ready for years of active nightlife!

# 33 | LIZARDS

*L*izards are great! But they're not for everyone.

On the other hand, caring for lizards presents a unique challenge, as well as a window onto a different sort of lifestyle and existence. Numerous different sorts of lizards are kept in captivity, including plant eaters and meat eaters. Partly because of the aesthetics of feeding prey to meat eating lizards and partly because of husbandry challenges, iguanas have until recently been the most commonly kept lizard in Canada. The kind I most often see in my practice is the green iguana; this chapter will focus on that species.

Common (or green) iguanas come from sub-tropical Central and South America. They are usually quite shy, and although they can climb and swim well they are not good at running long distances. That is why in the wild they are often found sitting on branches overhanging water. Anything frightening comes along and SPLASH—the iguana is off, swimming to a less dangerous place. Iguanas are mainly plant eating, and spend much time sunning themselves. Because of these characteristics, an ideal temperature range for an iguana is 28 to 33 degrees Celsius with a humidity greater than 50 percent. Branches should always be available to climb on, ideally in areas of direct sunlight, and clean water should always be available. In places where it is too cold to set up this type of environment outside it is best mimicked in a large terrarium with special reptile ultraviolet lamps. Over time, these bulbs wear out and produce less beneficial radiation than is needed, so replace them every six months or so.

Feed should consist of a wide variety of vegetables and greens, chopped into bite-sized pieces. Calcium rich vegetables such as turnip and beet greens, Swiss chard, spinach, romaine lettuce, parsley and dandelions are an important part of the diet. Frozen mixed vegetables are also a useful source of dietary plant matter. Although iguanas are plant-eating reptiles they can eat small amounts of protein type food such as cooked white chicken, tuna (canned and packed in water), cooked egg, or lean hamburger. In growing iguanas such protein sources can make up about 15 percent of the diet. In mature adults (over three years of age) they should not make up more than 5 percent of dietary intake. Young iguanas should eat daily while older ones may eat only a few times per week. Supplementation with a vitamin/mineral supplement containing calcium is a necessity, to help prevent bone problems.

One of the most common diseases I see in iguanas has to do with calcium deficiency. The calcium level in the body relates to the level of vitamin D made by the skin, which requires direct sunlight to do its job. Again, the use of artificial sun lamps made for reptiles is essential here, but even the best ones offer only about 2 percent of the ultraviolet exposure that direct sunlight does. That is why calcium-rich vegetables are so important in the diet, and a vitamin-mineral supplement is a requirement too. You may also give liquid calcium, available in some pharmacies, at a rate which varies by species, body size and dietary calcium intake. Theoretically, it is possible to give an iguana an overdose of calcium, but I have never seen that to be a problem in iguanas kept indoors.

As with all pets, it is a good idea to request a veterinary check up prior to the purchase of any iguana. Especially when groups of iguanas or other reptiles live together, disease can be devastating. The most common diseases seen among captive reptiles are due to improper husbandry, including improper diet or a dirty environment. Other common conditions include bacterial infections, parasite infestations, metabolic disease, and injuries. Several intestinal diseases of reptiles can be spread to humans, so proper diagnosis and treatment is very important. Remember to wash your hands after handling your lizard! Your veterinarian or local herpetologist can help with more specific information and advice.

# REPTILES

$\mathscr{R}$eptiles are great! But they're not for everyone.

On the other hand, because of their seemingly laid back nature and often unusual habitats, lifestyles, and physical characteristics, they can make ideal pets for anyone interested in a different sort of animal. Providing of course that he or she is willing to make the necessary arrangements to keep that pet healthy and happy. Reptiles kept in captivity vary widely. They include a wide range of sizes, from the anole that weighs a few grams to the 50-kilogram monitor lizard and from the 4-cm gecko to the 13-meter boa. Reproductively speaking they range from the skink that gives birth to one live offspring at a time to the turtle that lays more than a hundred eggs per clutch. Longevity wise they range from the Parson's chameleon who lives less than a year to the tortoise that will outlive generations of owners.

As mentioned in the last chapter on iguanas, we are severely limited in our ability to provide proper environments for our reptile friends in northern climates, where these pets need to be kept indoors. Several types of reptiles are nonetheless growing in popularity, including bearded dragons, snakes, and water turtles. Each of these species has different management requirements; the successful keeping of reptiles is dependent on mimicking the natural habitat as closely as possible. In this chapter we will take a look at snakes and turtles.

Even within the broad categories of both snake and turtle there are an amazing number of species, including water dwellers and landlubbers. Most turtles I see in practice are water turtles (usually red-eared sliders) and most snakes are land snakes (usually boas, pythons, corn and king snakes).

The following comments refer to these species—remember, there are big differences in ecological habitat and dietary requirements among the species. Before buying any reptile it is wise to research that particular species to see if its husbandry requirements (temperature, humidity, space, lighting, sanitation, etc.) can be met.

Ideal housing for both snakes and turtles maintains a heat gradient so they can seek out an area of preferred optimum temperature. I often see such pets become ill as a result of being kept in too cold an environment. For turtles the temperature should range from 25 to 30 degrees Celsius; with snakes aim for a range of 28 to 35 degrees. Obviously, supplemental heat is required in both cases. One of the best ways to increase temperature is to use a heat lamp (or more than one) separated from the enclosure by at least 5 centimeters. Be sure there is sufficient air circulation to avoid overheating; use a thermometer in the animals' living area and monitor it carefully. Always have a source of clean water available for drinking or soaking because the humidity in our houses is often too low for reptilian comfort!

Most pet snakes eat on dry land, and large ones usually feed only a few times per month. Preferred food items include small mammals, birds, and (I hesitate to add) other reptiles too! I recommend whole killed prey for diet, but it can be quite challenging to get pet snakes to eat. Some are finicky eaters and require special food preparation or presentation. I have dealt with a number of snakes that refused to eat for more than a year!

Meat eating turtles also should eat whole killed prey, and aquatic types often prefer fish and slugs, worms and sometimes insects. Some tasty greens such as pond weeds or algae (some turtles will eat lettuce) can make up a small portion of the diet. Turtles usually like to eat in the water, but they also pass stool and urine there! When the living area contains only a small body of water, it can become dirty very quickly.

Contamination of feeding areas is a common problem that is preventable only by special management. Generally, it is advisable to feed adult turtles in the water at least several times per week, and to do so in a feeding area separate from the living area.

As with any pet, it is a good idea to get a veterinary check-up prior to the purchase of a snake or turtle. Be aware that people can catch disease from reptiles as well as from other pets, and it is always wise to perform routine disease prevention measures. See your veterinarian or local herpetologist for more advice—your reptilian pet may live with you for decades!

# 35

# RABBITS

*R*abbits are great! But they're not for everyone.

On the other hand, what other animal is so soft and cuddly? There is nothing quite like stroking the soft ears of a gentle rabbit. There are many types of rabbits available for pets, from small to large and shorter to longer haired, and even shorter to longer eared rabbits! Most domestic rabbits can trace their lineage back to European roots; this has implications for feeding, housing, and husbandry.

Rabbits can withstand fairly extreme weather variations but do best in cooler temperatures. They can be left outside in the winter only when exposed to gradual weather changes throughout autumn. This allows them to develop thick warm coats. Rabbits that live indoors however, cannot tolerate the dramatic temperature changes that may happen if they suddenly find themselves outdoors. Many people keep rabbits in the house and when that is the case, have them housed in plastic or metal hutches. Flooring may be newspapers or paper towels or wood chips, but don't use aromatic wood chips such as cedar or even pine, for they can cause skin irritation and respiratory problems. Rabbits do need more exercise than is afforded by small hutches but should not be left unattended in the house, where electric cords and other hazards are present.

Two of the more common and more easily preventable health problems seen in rabbits are dental disease and gastric stasis syndrome. Although there are other factors involved, both problems can largely be prevented by feeding good quality timothy grass hay as the main diet source. This hay promotes chewing which helps wear teeth down (rabbits' teeth grow continually and can cause big problems if they overgrow). It also provides a high fiber nutritional intake (necessary for proper function of stomach and intestines). Although commercial rabbit pellets may be fed as a small part of the diet they should be used more as treats. High fiber pellets are better. Feeding rabbits poor quality pellets and not enough hay can lead to dental and intestinal problems. It often results in fat rabbits that suffer from obesity related health problems too. Of course fresh water should always be available, and feeding small amounts of a variety of fresh greens every day helps to provide balanced nutrition.

Rabbits are prey animals by nature and can be very nervous. They can also be quite aggressive, especially if not neutered or spayed. They need careful handling because their back legs are so strong that if frightened and not supported well, kicking of the back legs can result in a broken back and paralysis. Because of their nature, and despite the fact that rabbits can be delightful, I do not recommend rabbits as starter pets or for young children. Rabbits do well as solitary individuals and often live to about seven years of age.

As always, health exams prior to purchase of a rabbit are recommended, and washing hands after handling rabbits is a good idea. Rabbits themselves are very hygienic and unless they run into health problems usually never need bathing or grooming. Ideally, keep rabbits in a quiet part of the house, to reduce their stress. It goes the other way too—caring for rabbits and watching and stroking them can help reduce our own stress levels!

# 36

# GUINEA PIGS

*G*uinea pigs are great! But they're not for everyone.

On the other hand, for people looking for a good starter pet for children, I can't think of a better one.

Guinea pigs are sturdy, personable little creatures that generally live about 5-8 years of age, and are not very intensive as far as financial and time input required to keep them happy. Appropriate housing includes cages that are quite large (1/2 x 1 meter or larger, and 1/2 meter high), with plastic bottom and wire sides. Gravity fed water bottles, clean flooring and fresh good quality hay are the minimum requirements; an area to hide in also helps keep them calm, especially if housed in high traffic areas of the house. Substrate on the floor of the cage may be print-free newspaper, paper towel or wood chips. The chips are available at many pet stores; choose aspen if possible and stay away from cedar chips, for its aromatic resins can lead to foot and respiratory problems. Guinea pigs like what we consider room temperature, so there is no special need for additional heating or lighting. They are not nocturnal, so that fits in nicely with our schedules too. In addition, they are often quite sociable. They can be very happy as solitary animals, but also do well in groups (it is best to have all of the same gender together though, unless you are planning on multiplication). When the weather is nice, guinea pigs enjoy going outside and running around in the grass (which is fine as long as there has been no pesticide or herbicide use). Do keep an eye on them at all times or put them in an escape-proof enclosure for they are sure to wander off when given the chance.

Guinea pigs are a prey species and frighten easily. However, they tolerate gentle handling very well and some become quite friendly—they each have their own characteristics! The dental issues mentioned in the last chapter on rabbits equally apply to guinea pigs, so provision of hay as main diet source (with very few pellets used as supplementary feeding only) is important. They can also be fed a wide variety of fresh vegetables, which they usually eat with gusto! Just like other pets, they may well enjoy unhealthy foods, and get fat if we let them. Overweight guinea pigs are susceptible to the same heart, joint and other problems that overweight people are so don't let them down by giving inappropriate foods please. Guinea pig hay racks are available and useful for keeping hay off the ground and reducing wastage. Several days worth of hay and water can be placed in a guinea pig cage at a time, making maintenance of the animal quite simple. Usually a complete cleaning of the living area on a weekly basis is sufficient.

Guinea pigs can get gastric stasis as mentioned for rabbits in the previous chapter, but other diseases are rare in solitary animals. Skin problems and infected lymph nodes are not uncommon, but when the environment is always clean such difficulties are minimized. Common respiratory and eye infections are also largely prevented by regular cleaning and good air quality.

Two species specific conditions that guinea pig owners need to be aware of are pubic bone fusion and vitamin C deficiency. Female guinea pigs that remain unmated by about 8 months of age will develop fused pubic bones as they mature. This means that the normal movement of pubic bones necessary at time of birthing is not possible in older guinea pigs that have not had litters by the time they are nine or ten months old. This is extremely important to remember when guinea pigs of both genders are housed together. A successful breeding of an older virgin guinea pig sow is a death sentence—cesarean section surgeries are the only way to save the mother and her young in such a situation. I recommend guinea pigs be spayed and neutered by the time they are 4-6 months of age, partly for this reason.

Secondly, although many animals can synthesize their own vitamin C in body cells, guinea pigs are like humans in that they cannot. Without supplementation of vitamin C (necessary for cell wall integrity in all cells of the body), guinea pigs will develop scurvy, an illness manifested in many parts of the body including skin and gastro-intestinal tract. Supplemental vitamin C is available in chewable tablets (give about 50 mg per day to each adult) or you can add it to the drinking water at the rate of about 600 mg/liter water.

Guinea pigs too can enrich the quality of our lives to a far greater degree than we enrich theirs. When children and guinea pigs get together, one can often hear squeals of delight from both.

That just goes to show—pets are great!

# POSTSCRIPT

*I* wish to thank all those who helped me by reviewing the stories that make up this little book, especially my mother Dr. Anne Kwantes, who has a lot more publishing experience than I. A few reviewers found some stories a little depressing, when they ended in death of the pet. But of course life does not end in death! So if you feel sad after reading any of these tales then I have not done justice to its main character, because each is a joyful celebration of life given, received, and shared.

If you have any feedback for me after reading these stories, I would like to hear it. If you have tales of pets who have given you joy, deepened your level of compassion, or influenced your spiritual journey, I would also like to hear from you. Please e-mail me at vetmedinc@aol.com

ISBN 142515997-4

9 781425 159979